# Off The Beadin' Path
### Discovering Your Own Creative Trail
### of Bead Embellishment

Nancy Eha

Creative Visions Press, St. Paul, Minnesota

Off The Beadin' Path is bound with a
stay open binding. Push firmly down on
the inner spine of the open book.

# Off The Beadin' Path
## Discovering Your Own Creative Trail
## of Bead Embellishment

By Nancy Eha

Published by:

## Creative Visions Press

3898 Dellview Avenue
St. Paul, Minnesota 55112   USA
(612) 633-3668   FAX (612) 633-2107

10 9 8 7 6 5 4 3 2 1
Printed in the United States of America
Library of Congress Catalog Card Number: 96-93101

**Library of Congress Cataloging-in-Publication Data**
Eha, Nancy
      Off The Beadin' Path: Discovering Your Own Creative Trail of
      Bead Embellishment / Nancy Eha
      144 p.  23 cm.
      Includes bibliographical references
      ISBN  0-9656476-0-9
      1. Beadwork  I. Title

Every effort has been made to ensure that all the information in this book is accurate. However, due to differing conditions, tools, and individual skills, the author and publisher cannot be responsible for any injuries, losses, and other damages which may result from the direct or indirect use of information in this book.

# About The Author

For as long as she can remember, Nancy Eha has been enticed by anything created by hand and in awe of the inventiveness of it's creator. Her heritage includes several ancestors who were compulsive creators, inventing and creating for the sheer pleasure of working with their hands.

After experimenting with numerous needle arts over a twenty year period, Nancy is most stimulated by beads. She is lured to the color and texture of beads, but even more by the infinite creative possibilities beads provide. She tends to create large labor intense pieces experimenting with her own numerous intuitive and inventive beading processes. Most often her art is expressive. She creates beadwork not for mere decorative purposes, but uses beads as her voice to reflect her view of self and society. Her main goal in creating is to continually challenge herself to grow as a beadwork artist. A secondary goal is to exhibit her art in textile and beadwork shows, sharing with others the art of beadwork.

As a dynamic workshop instructor, she stresses both exploring beading techniques and the development of the individual's creative process. The inspiration for this book came from Nancy's students. She was frequently asked for the name of a book to support one's quest to free his/her creative energy and provide instructions for the beading techniques she has developed. As that book did not exist, Nancy was determined to make Off The Beadin' Path a reality.

In addition to being a workshop instructor, lecturer, and author, beads have led Nancy to serve as exhibit advisor and researcher of antique beaded bags. She is a grant recipient and was provided funding to research and document one of her slide lectures: "Beady Eyed Visionaries, Expressive Beadwork Artists." Her beadwork has been featured in numerous national juried shows, and has won several awards. She has developed over 100 hours of beadwork workshop curricula. Nancy's greatest joy, aside from exploring with beads, is teaching workshops and witnessing her students' creativity unfold.

Nancy Eha has tried to make this book as clear and accurate as possible. Self published with limited resources, Off The Beadin' Path was never intended to be a glossy "coffee" table art book. Instead, it is a workbook to guide and encourage you as you explore your own personal trail of creative self discovery. Nancy welcomes your comments and photos or slides of your inspired work. Send all correspondence to Nancy Eha, c/o Creative Visions Press, 3898 Dellview Avenue, St. Paul, MN 55112.

## Dedication

To fellow Minnesotan and explorer Ann Bancroft, first woman to reach both the North and South Poles.

Ann has encouraged me to "Chase my dreams!"

# Table of Contents

# Table of Contents

## Appendix (con'd)

## Order Forms

# Introduction

# Preparing For The Journey

*Do not follow where the path may lead.*
*Go instead where there is no path and leave a trail.*

**Unknown**

**Welcome to your journey <u>Off The Beadin' Path</u>!** The goal of this book is to guide you and encourage you to go where no other beader has been: Your own unique journey of creative self-discovery!

<u>Off The Beadin' Path</u> will help you reclaim your creative nature, give you the courage to leave your city of comfort, and dare you to go into the wilderness of your intuition. You will discover your creative self as you take part in your evolution from a beading craftsperson to a beadwork artist.

On the first four trails, you will be introduced to ideas and be guided through exercises which will help you become a life-long creative explorer. As you begin to blaze your own trail of creative self-expression, you will discover and learn how to use these trailblazing techniques to unblock the flow of your creative energy. Each of the first four trails consists of an introductory reading with homework

1

exercises to free your creative spirit. You will need a notebook, which I call a Discovery Journal, for notes, sketches, and "homework" assignments.

These four trails are designed to be read one at a time, one chapter a week. Read and do the exercises before you start experimenting with the beading portions, or read and bead your way through the book. Either way, leave your beadin' path and allow yourself to experience your creative energy.

Read and think about each trail, do the activities, and seek out a supportive friend who can share in your struggles and progress. I highly recommend that you have a *supportive* friend or group to share with. The emphasis is on support. You may need to share this book or encourage your friend to buy his/her own copy to make your all important support system work.

On the remaining eight trails, new and innovative fabric beading techniques are introduced. Again, you will be encouraged to blaze your own creative trail as you explore numerous Challenges following each beading technique.

Allow yourself time to become familiar with each new trail. Practice using the trail and give yourself ample time to learn and grow. Changing your attitude and behavior is never a "quick fix." Liken yourself to an ocean liner. A motor boat operator need only reach back, grab the outboard motor handle, and jerk the handle to turn. Changing the course of a small boat does not require much planning, skill, or patience. It's course is quickly altered. In contrast, an ocean liner must slowly navigate and maneuver into a new direction. It takes planning, awareness, patience and much skill to change it's course successfully. Remember, you are a large and powerful vessel!

There will be times when your efforts will seem uncomfortable and awkward. The uncomfortable feelings you are experiencing are necessary for change to occur. In time, your new attitudes and behaviors will become second nature as they are integrated into your creative process.

Let the journey begin!

**What Madame Oolong Saw for Caldonia**
Kelly Johnson
*Back Stitch, Lazy Stitch, Couching*

3

**Bead Nicks**
Kae Krueger
*Numerous stitches from Trail 6 and Trail 7*

Trail 1

# Exploring Possibilities

*Every child is born an artist.*

*The problem is how to remain an artist once he grows up.*

*Pablo Picasso*

**You cannot be taught to be creative.** Deep inside all of us is abundant creativity. The truth is, we are all far more creative than we let ourselves believe. You only need to get out of the way and let your creative energy work through you.

I have observed a major difference between adults and young children. Adults continually question whether they have the potential to become creative. Children are naturally inquisitive, curious and playful. When presented with art materials young children do not stand back and ask, "What is the right way to create with these materials?", or "What should my completed project to look like?". Children immediately involve themselves with the materials at hand and become immersed in the process of creating. Adults hesitate, afraid that they will be wrong.

We all were once children. What has happened to our spontaneity, our joy of discovery? Could it be that we have been systematically directed away from the natural process of creativity? I find it ironic that my struggles directing children's natural creativity was the reason for which I left classroom teaching twenty years ago, and now helping adults unblock their creative energy has propelled me back to teaching.

Allowing children to be inquisitive and self-directed in their learning process was like holding a can of marbles at waist height and dumping them on a desk top. They were noisy, took different paths, and were actively involved in learning by bouncing from idea to idea. Unfortunately, this was in contrast to the administrative goals of quiet classrooms, the same curriculum for every child, and the high value placed on standardized test results achieved through "traditional" teaching methods.

I have seen recent studies where the value of incorporating arts into all subject matter has increased the amount and ease of learning. I know of a few schools that are using the art integrated approach in the teaching of some or all subject matter. Let's hope this trend of validating the creative process as part of the total educational process continues.

Children who are self-directed, exploratory learners, are "off the beaten path" of the family and school focus which is on product or outcome. Due to the negative media stereotype that artists are unstable, shiftless, drug addicted, and will never make a "decent" living, parents may directly or indirectly discourage their children from becoming artists.

Comments such as: "Make your picture look like mine.", "That's not right, a clay pot should look like this.", or "We can't use those art supplies, they are too messy." can make children hesitant to continue on their own trail of creative self-expression. As children, we hear negativity about artists and doubts about our ability to be creative from the adults who have the greatest impact on our life choices. By the time we become adults, we have developed our own critical inner voice. Your inner critic keeps you on the "safe" path by repressing your creative desires and conforming to others' expectations. We are all more creative than we let ourselves believe. You can allow yourself to be more creative than you believe you are.

You were born with an infinite and abundant amount of creative potential. There is an unlimited amount of both creativity and success in this world, enough for everyone. The sum total of all creative energy is not kept at one huge creative power plant. If one person uses creative energy, it doesn't decrease his or her supply or anyone else's. There is no competition for creative energy.

Releasing your personal creativity is allowing yourself to experiment and use free speculation of the materials of your chosen art form. In the movie, "Medicine Man", Sean Connery's character states, "Science is the process of eliminating possibilities." In contrast, *creativity is the process of exploring possibilities.* Beadwork is an art. It is not a science. There is not one right answer but many possible answers to explore.

To unblock your creative energy and let it flow back into your life, you must allow yourself the time to speculate, experiment, and PLAY. We all lead busy lives, and the technology that was to make more free time to enjoy has only sped up our pace and increased our time commitments. Take control. Go get your calendar and make an appointment to play with your beads. Take a Discovery Journey. You are telling yourself you will do it, but get the calendar and do it now!

**This week's homework assignment:**
For the next seven days, mark on your calendar a specific time(s) to take yourself on a Discovery Journey. On your Discovery Journey, focus on the *process* of creating, not on the product you produce.

Clear a table or a spot on the floor and take out all of your beading supplies. Okay, if you have a beadaholic size collection, take out a bushel basketful. Include in these supplies familiar items such as beads, findings, and fabric scraps. Also, add materials you usually don't include in your beadwork. These supplies might include: yarn, ribbon, wire, corks, straws, broken tile, bottles, sea shells, assorted papers and anything you can think of. Remember, your focus is not on what you are making, it is on what you are learning as you play and create with the materials at hand.

The Discovery Journey begins as you arrange, attach and combine the materials at hand in ways you never dreamed of or never felt safe doing. This is not a test or competition. The only goal you have is to discover new techniques, processes and combinations.

As you continue on your Discovery Journey, start a Discovery Journal. Purchase a notebook or sketch pad and jot down your new discoveries. It will help you remember if you draw, write an explanation, or tape a sample on the pages. Your entries may range from something as simple as orange and purple are exciting together, to more complex ideas. Just play and record your discoveries. Creativity is the process of exploring possibilities!

# Trail 2

**Beads of Wisdom**

# Soothing Your Inner Critic

*Judging your early artistic efforts is artistic abuse.*
*Julia Cameron*

**What does your inner critic say to you?** Your worst critic is yourself. You will think and say things to yourself that are much more abusive than any other person would dare to say to you. Your inner critic will make every attempt to keep you "safe" from creative risk and creative fulfillment.

In order to calm your inner critic, you must first be aware of what it is saying to you. When you were on your Discovery Journey, did you hear your inner voice telling you that you were no good at this creative stuff, that you would never be any good, and were stupid for wasting your time trying?

Everyone, no matter how successful, has an inner critic to deal with on an on-going basis. Left unchecked, it can zap your creative energy. The good news is that by actively listening and talking back, it becomes less and less powerful.

The first step in silencing your inner critic is to listen to your inner critic as you bead or do any creative endeavor. When you hear negative thoughts about yourself, your skill, or the creative process, jot them down in your Discovery Journal. Notice I said jot *them* down. Put aside what you are doing, and write down what you are hearing every time you hear your inner critical voice.

## WHAT DOES YOUR NEGATIVE INNER CRITIC SAY TO YOU?

1.

2.

3.

4.

5.

6.

Once you have a list of negative messages, the next step is to think of a positive comeback to calm this abusive authoritarian voice. If you choose, you can call these positive responses, affirmations. For example, my most prevalent abusive thought is: "Why are you wasting your time doing beadwork? There is no money in it. You should be doing something to earn money instead." (Can you tell I was raised to be product oriented and to value my self-image by my earnings?) My current soothing response to my inner critic is: "Contentment is worth more than money."

Very few negative thoughts will be calmed the first time you counter in a positive response. Most issues will be hard to overcome, but they can be defused. Your inner critic has been active most of your life. Like all learned behaviors and attitudes, it will take time to redirect your negative thoughts. It will get easier.

To support your efforts as you begin, I have listed some positive, soothing, self-talk comebacks. The plan is to listen to your own destructive dialogue and respond with a positive self-image supporting affirmation. I call these nurturing responses, "Beads of Wisdom." Some of my "Beads of Wisdom" may work for your issues. Or, you may have to devise your own "Beads of Wisdom" to calm your inner critic.

## Beads of Wisdom

Leap and a net will appear.

There is no such thing as a mistake, only opportunities for further exploration.

Judging your early artist efforts is artistic abuse.

It is impossible to look good and get better at the same time.

Focus on the creative process, not the outcome.

A discovery is an accident meeting a prepared mind.

Success is 10% inspiration and 90% perspiration.

To live a creative life, we must lose our fear of being wrong.

Contentment is worth more than money.

**This week's homework assignment:**

Fold one page of your Discovery Journal vertically in half. Then open the page so it is flat again. You have just made two columns by folding.

Go on a beading Discovery Journey. Experiment with techniques you know or are learning. Put down your art every time you hear your inner critical voice. In the right column, list your negative, creative, energy-zapping dialog. In the left column, write down a "Bead of Wisdom" to counteract each negative attitude you have recorded.

Each time you take out your beadwork, open your Discovery Journal to the page on which you have recorded your personal "Beads of Wisdom". Review this page often. Old habits die hard!

Keep adding documentation of your creativity-zapping dialogue and your soothing "Beads of Wisdom" in your Discovery Journal.

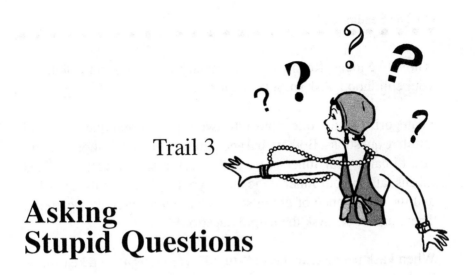

# Trail 3

# Asking
# Stupid Questions

*When you ask a dumb question, you get a smart answer.*

**Aristotle**

**Have you ever wanted to quench your curiosity with a question, but were afraid to ask it?** Immediately, your inner critic took over and told you, "Don't ask that! You will really look stupid. The answer is so apparent that everyone else knows the answer but you." Your excitement to learn was squashed. Your inner critic made you tow the line, not allowing you to be vulnerable and not allowing your curiosity to add to the joy of living. Asking stupid questions enriches your life and gives you new ideas to use in free association as you create.

Asking a stupid question is really asking an inquisitive question. Have the courage to be naive and the information you receive will alter and expand your perspective on your life and on your art.

The term naive is usually associated with children. In our culture, adults who are considered naive might be considered immature or vulnerable. However, we are talking about being more child-like in our gathering of information, not a total transformation back to childhood. We need to become comfortable with these child-like qualities in the exploration of the creative process and in developing

13

innovative ideas. Regain the spontaneity, curiosity, and wonder of your childhood. Ask stupid questions!

I categorize stupid questions into two types, verbal questions and intuitive questions. Both verbal and intuitive stupid questions require you to calm your inner critic and to ask a stupid question. This means talk to your inner critic about your right to ask the question and the importance of doing so to release your creative potential. Then, just do it. Ask the stupid question!

When I ask people curious or "stupid" questions, they take time to think about an answer and seem genuinely complimented that I asked them the question. In our fast-paced, technical world, stupid questions indicate that you care enough about the person, their knowledge, skills and life experiences to ask a question. After answering my stupid question, I have even been told that I made their day by asking!

When an opportunity appears, ask a stupid question. Ask the stupid question, even though your critical inner dialogue tells you not to. I have asked of a flamboyant stranger with a dog, "Do you think your dog could be a vegetarian?" and to a bank teller, "Did you have to go to a special school to count the bills so fast?" Not only do you participate in the joy of learning, but asking questions helps you develop the skill of free association. Free association of ideas will unblock your creative energy.

Intuitive stupid questions are the pairing of two different ideas in your mind. If you are continually asking stupid questions, you will have an endless supply of new information to pair with information you already have stored in your memory. By pairing ideas, you allow yourself to explore and develop an abundance of creative combinations.

**This week's homework assignment:**
Challenge yourself to ask a minimum of one stupid question a day.
Go for extra credit and ask all the stupid questions you can think of!
Start a section in your Discovery Journal entitled: "I Learn By Asking
Stupid Questions." Record any piece of information you learned
from having the courage to ask.

Take the information you learned from one stupid question and use
it in a rough sketch of a possible beading project. Use your
imagination. There are no wrong answers.

Continue to listen to your inner critic. Write down every negative
remark you tell yourself. Then write a calming "Bead of Wisdom"
in your Discovery Journal to soothe your inner critic.

**Ribbon Flowers With Bead Embellishment**
Elinor Auge

**Humming Birds In Columbine**
Jo Wood
*Back Stitch and Couching*

Trail 4

# Listening
# From Within

*Unless you try to do something beyond what you
have already mastered, you will never grow.*

*Ronald E. Osborn*

The process of pairing two pieces of information and stupid questioning gives you the courage to free associate ideas, techniques, and skills together in your beadwork. This free association results in your own unique creative discoveries.

I call this process intuitive beading. Intuition is a right brain function. This is in contrast to analytical decisions, a left brain function. You are using your intuition when you feel or believe you will get a desirable outcome. Yes, this is creative risk taking, but your beads can't hurt you. You will never grow creatively if you do not take risks with your beadwork. What is the worst that can happen? You'll discover something new!

By starting a section entitled Idea Keeper in your Discovery Journal, you can record your ideas, processes, and problems for future use. I know we all think we can remember these good ideas, but unless you record ideas as you have them, you will not remember.

The Idea Keeper is divided in two sections, ideas and projects. In the idea section make notes or drawings of inspirations and ideas. I find I am visually orientated and so sketches are my best memory jogger.

In the project section, record sketches for future or on-going projects. I often sketch and fine tune my project ideas five times or more during the construction process. Be flexible. As new ideas come to you or you realize the limitations of your materials, revise your sketch. Beads are appealing for their endless creative possibilities but they have inherent limitations. Beadwork cannot always become a literal translation of your sketch or desired outcome. Remember, creativity is the process of exploring possibilities!

**This week's homework assignment:**
Take yourself on a weekly Discovery Date. Make a list of ten things you enjoy doing. Pick one, schedule in the time on your calendar and do it. Your Discovery Date does not have to be art related. It could be enjoying flower gardens, a movie, or anything *you* would like to do. It is best to go alone. If you go alone, you can focus on yourself and your reactions to the activity, not your companion's reactions. You can interact with the environment without distraction. It is creatively healthy to become comfortable with solitude. Going alone will help you relax, listen, and observe.

Take your Discovery Journal with you and record ideas in the Idea Keeper section that you could incorporate with your bead work. It can be as simple as observing and recording the texture of cement. Or, your ideas generated from your Discovery Date can be more complex, an innovative design concept, a new beading technique, or a subject for a future beading project.

# Preparation
# of Materials

## Preparation Check List

Do I need to:

\_\_\_\_ 1. Check beads for color fastness?

\_\_\_\_ 2. Pre-wash fabric?

\_\_\_\_ 3. Use nylon or natural fiber thread?

\_\_\_\_ 4. Use a beading needle to pass through bead holes?

\_\_\_\_ 5. Use a hoop or canvas fabric stretcher?

REMEMBER: Use double thread whenever possible.

**I cannot over emphasize the importance of thinking ahead in the preparation and suitability of your chosen materials.** I know you are eager to begin and complete your project. For all the hours you work on your beadwork projects, you deserve to have a good outcome! If you don't have time to do it right, when are you going to have time to do it over?

## Supplies

## Beads

If you think you might need to clean your finished work in the future or it will be exposed to wetness, you must test your beads for color fastness. Certain shades of glass beads are dyed on the surface. You may have noticed your hands, thread, or bead plate turning the color of those bright red beads that you loved for their vivid shade of red. Some bead surfaces may not be dyed and are not a concern. Other beads have dye applied to their center lining and are called color lined beads. Color lined beads may not be color fast. To save yourself frustration later, take time to test a sample of all the beads you plan to use before you start the project.

Be sure to buy enough beads for your project before you start. Beads, like cloth or yarn, are produced in dye lots. The colors change from lot to lot. You may go back to buy additional beads and find the color is not the same.

## Testing Beads For Color Fastness

If your finished work will be **hand or machine washed**, or will come in contact with water:
1. Put one tablespoon of dish detergent in a cereal bowl and add approximately 1/2 cup of water.
2. Put several beads of every color and type you will be using in the solution.
3. Soak for two hours or longer.
4. Drain and rinse in a strainer, using cheese cloth in the strainer.
5. Do not use any beads that have lost color or changed color.

If your finished work will be **dry cleaned**:
1. Sew several beads of each color that you plan to use on the inside lining of a garment that is dry cleanable.
2. Have the garment dry cleaned.
3. Do not use any beads that have lost color or changed color.

# Thread

The thread of choice for most beaders is a nylon thread known by it's trade name Nymo. Nymo is a nylon thread whose fibers lay parallel. My personal favorite is a nylon thread known as Silamide, a trade name for button hole twist thread. It has long been used by tailors. Silamide's pre-waxed fibers are twisted together. I find Silamide superior for all types of beadwork using size 11 seed beads or larger.

Silamide is sold in size A. Nymo is sold in sizes OO, O, A, B, and D. OO is the finest and D is the thickest. For beading on fabric, I use Silamide size A and Nymo size D.

Silamide and Nymo are both nylon threads. If you were around back in the days when people ironed everything including sheets and underwear, you might remember scorching a slip or other nylon garment. The iron probably left a dark brown iron imprint on the spot of your indiscretion, as well as melting and shrinking the material around the iron imprint. If you will be ironing the garment or the project, do not use nylon thread. Use poly/cotton instead.

Threads used to secure beads are often a visible part of the work. Use a colored thread with a clear bead and the bead will take on the color of the thread. Colored threads used with semi-transparent beads can also change the bead color. The use of a contrasting thread can provide a unique beading outcome. If you want to minimize the visibility of the thread, use a color of thread close to the fabric color.

Always use a double thread. If one strand breaks, the other strand will hold your work until you can repair the break. To avoid tangles and knots, use no more than a two yard length of thread (one yard when doubled).

After doubling the two yards of thread to a one yard length, knot the tails together in a double knot. When you need to change threads,

21

knot your working thread tightly to the wrong side of the fabric.

Hint: To break an unwanted strung seed bead, position flat nose pliers near the edge of the bead and press shut. Applying pressure on the end on the bead will prevent the broken glass from cutting through the thread. It is important to *close your eyes or use safety glasses* to protect your eyes from flying glass pieces.

# Needles

Beading needles come in several sizes for use with different size beads. As size 11 seed beads are used in almost all the techniques in this book, use size 12 beading needles. Size 12 beading needles work well with size 14, 11, 10, 8 or larger bead. As with beads, the higher the number, the smaller the diameter of the needle.

It is important to use good quality needles. Purchase your needles at bead shops or through the mail from bead suppliers. It has been my experience that the beading needles sold in most fabric shops are not sized correctly. Often, a size 12 needle is too large to pass through the hole of a size 11 bead.

Beading needles are made in two lengths: short and long. Short needles are also know as Sharps. I find the size 12 short needles provide me with more control when picking up beads for most beadwork. Loom work requires longer needles.

I have observed beaders with large hands who can control long needles better than short needles. If you have large hands, you may find that your fingers take up almost all of the space on a short needle and leave you little space to put on the beads.

In my workshops, we do the hardest thing first: threading the needle. Needle threaders do not work as beading needle eyes are small in order to pass through the bead holes. Thread a minimum of three needles before starting a work session. Your eyes are fresh, and you can keep your momentum going as you change needles.

I use a three step process in threading a needle:
1. Wax the tip of any unwaxed thread by holding the last inch down on the beeswax and pulling the end over the wax surface. As Silamide is prewaxed, there is no need to wax it.
2. Pull the waxed end between the thumb and forefinger to flatten the fibers. Waxing and flattening will make the fibers stick together.
3. With a sharp scissors, cut the waxed and flattened end of the thread on a diagonal. Cutting on a diagonal will make a narrower point and make it easier to pass the thread through the eye of the needle.

By holding the thread 1/4" from the cut point and guiding the needle to the thread, you will have better control threading the needle. If necessary, repeat the waxing, flattening and cutting process. You may also find it helpful to use a magnifying glass when threading the needle.

Your needles will bend and sometimes break with use. It is best to buy ten or more at a time. A bent needle can be straightened and used again. With a toothless flat nose pliers, firmly slide the pliers up the shaft of the needle. Repeat until the needle is straight again.

Flat nosed pliers can also be used to pull a needle through a tight bead hole. Grasp the needle with the toothless flat nose pliers at the point of exit of the bead hole. Pull the needle firmly and slowly until the needle passes through the bead.

• • • • • • • • • • • • • • • • • • • • • • • • • • •

# Plates

Use a large white glass or ceramic plate to pour your beads onto. The white plate will let you see the true colors of your chosen beads and the slick surface will enable you to glide your beads onto your needle. For white or very pastel beads, use a black plate or paint a section black on the white plate. Mix your bead colors on the plate. This will help you see new color combinations.

Get into the habit of not touching the seed bead with your non-beading hand. Instead, position the needle into the hole and glide the seed bead onto the needle. You can pick up several beads on the needle one at a time. Then, tip the point of the needle upward to allow the beads to fall down the body of the needle and slide down onto the thread.

To prevent back and shoulder aches, elevate your plate to mid-chest level by putting magazines or a sturdy box under the plate. Sit close to the table and pull the elevated plate close to you. In this position, you will be bending from your neck, not your back. Be sure to stand up, walk, and stretch your body frequently. Some beaders set a timer to go off every hour for the purpose of regular stretches and exercise.

# Lighting

Good lighting is a necessity for beading. A minimum of a 75 watt bulb in a desk or elbow lamp should be used over your work. Natural lighting is preferred for viewing the true color of the beads and fabric. Halogen lighting is second best and lastly a light bulb. A halogen lamp, trade name Ott light, and a halogen light with a magnifier can be purchased at large office supply stores.

Some beaders use a large lighted magnifier which is worn around their neck or is attached to their light. Be prepared to buy, try and return several lamp and magnifying combinations before finding the best option for you.

Working with seed beads may necessitate a change in your glasses prescription. Some beaders purchase an inexpensive pair of reading glasses at a drug store just for beading. Your eyes, like your body, need to be given a break and exercised during beading sessions. Look up, outside or across the room every 15 minutes so your eyes can focus on different distances.

# Fabric Considerations

When you buy fabric, check the bolt end for washing recommendations. You need to consider both "natural" and "unnatural" shrinkage of any fabric you choose to use in your beadwork.

**"Natural" shrinkage** occurs when the fabric is washed. If there is even a chance you will at sometime wash this project, wash it! Wash all fabrics before you begin any stage of marking, cutting, or beading. Not only will the fabric shrink slightly, but this initial wash will remove any sizing surface finishes applied at the fabric mill.

**"Unnatural" shrinkage** is my term for what happens to your fabric as you bead on it. By pulling the thread too tight, your thread tension creates fabric ripples that change the size of the fabric piece. Fabric ripples will change the width and length of the piece you are working on and cause it to not lay flat. This can be a real problem if you have marked the pattern pieces you are beading on. When you later try to cut and sew the fabric into a finished project, the pieces will no longer be the proper size.

### Preservation of fabric shape.
Before any beading or hand sewing, I highly recommend you pull the fabric taut enough to keep it flat without stretching it. The horizontal and vertical threads should be kept in straight parallel lines. Yes, you must look closely. I have avoided using embroidery hoops, scrolls, and other contraptions in the past and have regretted it. These are a must if you have a predetermined fabric shape you need to retain for a successful outcome. For knit fabrics, you must baste Pellon or interfacing to the wrong side of the fabric before beading. Pellon will stabilize knits and keep them from stretching as you bead. *Pellon is a registered trademark of Freudenberg Nonwovens.*

# Securing The Fabric
**Hoops and scrolls** have limitations. Bead embellishment on fabric has more dimension and texture than needle arts such as crewel, cross stitch and embroidery. Once you bead on an area of fabric, you can no longer put the edge of a hoop over it nor wrap it into the scrolls. You cannot use hoops or scrolls if you want to move them from area to area for beading purposes. Hoops and scrolls are fine for smaller projects where you do not need to move the hoop or turn the scrolls. Caution: You may not be able to get as close to the hoop edge as you want. Before starting with a hoop, scroll or canvas stretcher, remember to leave a margin of fabric that will not need to be embellished.

**Canvas stretchers** can be purchased at art supply stores. They come in many precut lengths that are interchangeable. The lengths are attached at the corners. The frame is used to stretch canvases for painting or to hold fabric in place for beading. Use gloves to protect yourself from splinters as you push the corners together.

Choose frame lengths that are approximately *4-5 inches shorter on each side than your muslin base*. Caution: 4-5 inches on each side, not 4-5 inches shorter in total length. You will need these extra inches on *all sides* to fold over the frame, and fasten the muslin securely in place.

Before attaching your fabric to the muslin base, mark the beading design on your fabric, or make your pattern on tissue paper and pin it to the fabric after it is on the stretcher. You do not need to mark the design if you are exploring beading techniques and combinations. In that case, let your creativity direct you! Remember to leave the standard 5/8" plus an additional 1/8" seam allowance free of surface decoration when planning your beading design if you will be sewing pieces together with a sewing machine. You will need the standard 5/8" plus an additional 1/8" seam allowance to allow your sewing machine presser foot to clear your beadwork. Choose a presser foot that is as narrow as possible for better control sewing near your beadwork.

Attach your pre-washed fabric to a piece of muslin that will then be attached to the canvas stretcher. You can hand or machine baste the fabric in place on the muslin. The muslin should be large enough to be stapled or tacked to the top surfaces of the stretching frame.

Stretch the muslin enough to be flat, but not so much that your horizontal or vertical threads become unparallel. Have another person hold and gently stretch the muslin in place while you start at the *middle of opposite ends* and staple gun or thumb tack the fabric in place. Start at the middle of the opposite sides, then work outward. Secure the other two sides in the same manner. Be careful not to staple your fingers!

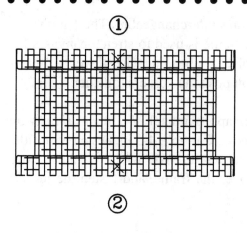

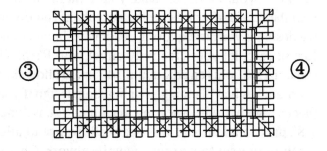

For instruction on building a wooden floor stand to hold your canvas stretchers, see pages 122-123.

When your surface embellishment is completed, remove the thumb tacks or staples. Use a screw driver or butter knife to get under the thumb tacks or staples and lift them off. You are now ready to cut out your pattern pieces and construct your project.

Once you have hand or machine stitched the pieces together to form your project, you can go back and bead on and near the seams. You will need to watch the thread tension as you hand sew in these areas. Keep the beads tight to the fabric but avoid a too tight thread tension which will make the material pucker.

# Bead Appliqué

The bead appliqué stitches on this trail have been in use for hundreds of years. However, prior to the introduction of glass seed beads by European explorers, Native Americans used dyed porcupine quills to embellish articles of clothing with quillwork.

Native Americans used bead appliqué to decorate garments for special occasions, not for daily wear. Traditional beadwork rarely served as mere decoration, but it formed an integral part of the culture for which it was designed. It was truly expressive beadwork expressing the artist's unique view of self and society.

Note: The term bead "appliqué" is interchanged with bead embroidery or bead sewing depending on the source of the information.

**Before beading:** READ PREPARATION CHECKLIST page 19.

### Illustration Key:

The long horizontal line_____ is the fabric.

The beads and thread above the fabric line indicate the right side of fabric.

The area below the fabric line is the wrong side of fabric.

The X is the knot.

These stitches are not worked on the edge of the fabric. They are worked on the interior area. If you are taking small stitches or working on heavy fabric, you may not need a hoop or canvas stretcher for the Appliqué Stitches in this chapter.

# Back Stitch

**Fig. 1**
(To outline, fill-in, or write words)

During my research, I found many variations of the basic Back Stitch technique in print. I choose to work the Back Stitch in the following manner:

**Fig. 1**

Knot the thread and pass the needle up to the right side of the fabric. Put 3 beads on the needle and push them down the thread to the fabric. Hold the beads down on the fabric, leaving little slack in the thread. Pass the needle down through fabric close to where the thread is coming out of bead 3. Bring the needle up to the right side, between bead 1 and 2, and pass it through bead 2 and 3. Put on 3 new beads and repeat the process.

The second pass through the beads keeps the beads close to the fabric and reinforces their position.

**Challenges:**

1. **Fig. 2.** Use larger beads which weigh more. Attach these beads one at a time to the fabric. To anchor these heavier beads you will need to go through each bead twice.

**Fig. 2.**

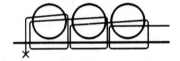

2. With a three seed bead sequence, make curved lines and shapes. You can control the curves by the location of the point you direct the needle down to the wrong side of the fabric after putting on the 3 bead sequence, and by the location of the point where you bring up the needle to the right side before making the second pass through beads 2 and 3.

# Lazy Stitch

**Fig. 3**

(Fill-in or full coverage with numerous channels of uniform width)

This stitch was often used to cover moccasins and cradle boards. When sewn on brain tanned animal hides, the needle does not pass entirely through the hide. Therefore, there is no thread on the wrong side or inside of the garment that is subject to wear and tear.

**Fig. 3**

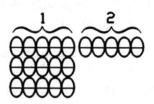

This an aerial view of the bead placement. Unlike the backstitch,the needle and thread do not go through the beads a second time. The beads are sewn on with 5 seed beads at a time row after row. The uniform horizontal seed bead rows will make 5 bead wide vertical channels. When you have a channel as long as you want, knot off and start at the top of the next channel as in **Fig. 3.**

Another option is to position the needle next to your last stitch and come up to the right side of the fabric and work bottom to top for the next row.

1. On the wrong side of the fabric, position the empty needle over the approximate width of one bead.

2. Pierce the fabric and bring the needle up to the right side of the fabric.

3. Start the next row of 5 beads. The beads should lay flat but should not be as tight to the fabric as the Back Stitch.

**Challenges:**

1. Use more than five beads per row. What happens? How could you use this variation?

2. **Fig. 4** Graph multicolored pattern(s), then work them in the Lazy Stitch.

3. Create texture with a Lazy Stitch "checker board" pattern. This technique can be adapted to create a basket weave pattern. How else could you use it?

**Fig. 4**

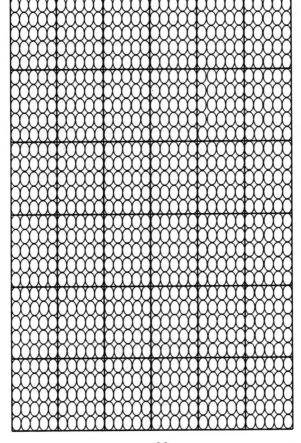

# Satin Stitch

**Fig. 5**

(Fill-in alone, or fill-in Back Stitch shape)

**Fig. 5**

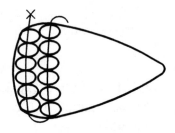

Think of the Satin Stitch as the Lazy Stitch worked in non-uniform rows to make an irregular shape. If need be, Back Stitch the longer rows to keep them tighter to the fabric.

**Challenges:**

1. For a textured look, vary the size of the beads in each row.

2. Design and bead a complex shape in which the Satin Stitch is worked in horizontal, vertical, and diagonal directions.

# Couching

Both **Fig. 6** and **Fig. 7** are aerial views of the right side of the fabric. **Fig. 6** shows the beads. **Fig. 7** shows the small stitches over the thread on the right side of the fabric.

(For long curvy lines which are less controlled than Back Stitch.)

**Fig. 6**

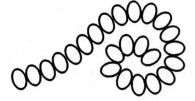

Put on a long row of seed beads on your thread. Make a continuous curvy line of beads on the fabric surface. Hold down the beads with the fingers from your non-beading hand.

**Fig. 7**

Pass the needle to the wrong side of the fabric, or use a second threaded needle. Come up to the right side between every 3 or 4 beads and take a small stitch *over the thread between the beads* on the right side of the fabric.

**Challenges:**

1. As you learn and work with these stitches, challenge yourself to develop art that contains your own personal symbolism.

2. Couch many strands of varying sizes of beads in a free form. Have some strands follow the contours of previous couching. Have others go off and form new contours. Try to replicate texture such as swirling water, wood grain, etc.

3. Give in to your Right Brain, do some intuitive beading! Let your beads speak to you, and go with the flow of what they want to do.

**I'm Not A Hot House Flower,**
**But More Of A Field Daisy** (Detail)
Ruth Satterlee
*Back Stitch, Couching*

# Creating Texture
# With Beads

What's your attraction to beads? Do you like the color, sparkle, or texture? Whatever your personal attraction to beads, you will find joy in these stitches!

On Trail 6, Bead Appliqué, we played it fairly safe and kept close to the fabric surface. On this trail, we will take more risks by adding beaded dimension and texture to the fabric.

Never fear, this is not brain surgery. Taking risks is necessary to release your creative potential. Leap and a net will appear!

For this trail, pick out 4 colors of size 11 beads that you believe *do not go together.* As you work the stitches, try combining 2 or 3 of these colors in each stitch.

**Before beading:** READ PREPARATION CHECKLIST page 19.

## Illustration Key:

The long horizontal line_____ is the fabric.

The beads and thread above the fabric line indicate the right side of the fabric.

The area below the fabric line is the wrong side of the fabric.

The "X" is the knot.

# Back Stitch Variations

**Fig. 1**

**Fig. 1**

Knot the thread and pass the needle up through the fabric to the right side as shown. Put on a large bead, 5 seed beads and a large bead on the thread. Hold the 2nd large bead on the fabric behind the 1st large bead so that the seed beads form a hump. Pass the needle down to the wrong side of fabric. *Pass the needle up to the right side of the fabric one large bead length in front of the 1st large bead. Put on 1 large bead and 5 seed beads on the needle and pass the needle down through the 1st large bead to the wrong side of the fabric. Repeat, starting at *. Continue working left to right.

**Challenge:**

1. **Fig. 2.** Use the same sequence, but eliminate the large beads and do not go through any bead twice. This variation is less stable because each hump stands alone and does not share a common bead with another hump.

Fig. 2

## Stop Stitch

Fig. 3

**Fig. 3**
The Stop Stitch and variations of the Stop Stitch all have something in common. They all have one or more beads called stop bead(s). The stop bead(s) keep the rest of the beads from falling off the fabric.

The Stop Stitch and variations show a knot before and directly after the stitch. The knots hold your beadwork in place, protecting it from unraveling if a thread should break. Use this double knot method if you are beading on a garment or object that will be subjected to wear. This also makes it easier to repair. This double knot system is not necessary on display pieces which are not worn.

After trying the Stop Stitch **Fig. 3,** try **Fig. 4** the Dangle Stop Stitch. Experiment by increasing the number of beads used as stop beads. For examples of this technique, see **Fig. 5** Picot Stop Stitch and **Fig. 6** Dangle Loop Stop Stitch.

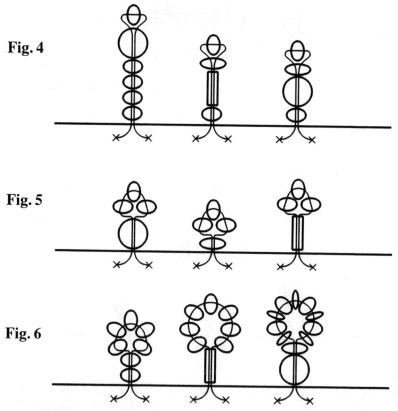

**Fig. 4**

**Fig. 5**

**Fig. 6**

If the stitches are not standing up and saluting, increase the tension by pulling the thread tighter. Hold down the remaining beads while the stop beads are pulled upward. Next, pull the needle and thread down tightly on the wrong side of the fabric.

# Off The Beadin' Path

Discovering Your Own
Creative Trail of
Bead Embellishment

Nancy Eha

# CHOOSE TO BE CREATIVE!
## 120+ page workbook includes:

- Readings and exercises to unleash your natural creative talents.

- Choosing the right supplies for success.

- Easy to learn beading stitches which will amaze and delight you with exotic results.

- New innovative hand sewn beading processes which not only embellish but shape and alter fabric surfaces as well.

- Step by step instructions with easy to understand diagrams.

- Packed with inspirational ideas for developing your own designs and projects.

**Signed Copies: $19.95 plus $3 Shipping**
**MN residents add $1.29 sales tax**

Sorry, no credit cards

**Creative Visions Press**
**3898 Dellview Avenue**
**St. Paul, MN 55112**

Photo by Candice Christensen

## Sticky Lollipops

**Fig. 7**

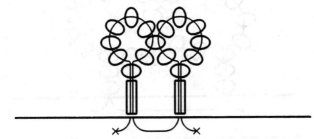

**Fig. 7**

Imagine sticky lollipops standing up on their sticks and stuck together by their edges. Now, construct this image with beads. The stick is a bugle bead and the lollipop is outlined with seed beads.

Sticky Lollipops are similar to the Dangle Loop Stitch on the preceding page. However, there are two differences. The first stop bead at the top of the bugle has the needle and thread pass through it twice. Second, the lollipops share one bead, so they stick together. Experiment with different numbers of beads in the loop and with different shared beads.

# Hand Cuffs

**Fig. 8**

Hand Cuffs are two Dangle Loop Stitches made entirely of seed beads. After beading the first hand cuff, thread on all the beads for the second loop. Then, pass the needle, thread, and beads through the loop of the first hand cuff before going down the base of the second hand cuff and to the wrong side of the fabric.

**Fig. 8**

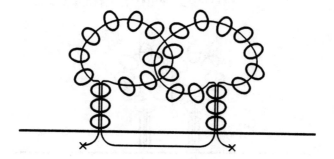

**Challenges:**

1. Link together more than two hand cuffs. What happens?

2. Replace all seed beads with all bugle beads.

3. Use different sizes of beads by themselves or in multiples.

4. Combine the Dangle Loop, Sticky Lollipop and Hand Cuff stitches in a Discovery Journey.

# Fence Stitches

**Fig. 9**

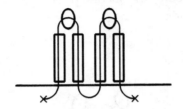

# Broken Fence Stitch

**Fig. 9**
The Fence Stitch is a variation of an edging stitch. We will explore edging stitches on Trail 8. As you make a line of Broken Fence, notice how it wobbles.

**Fig. 10**      **Secure Fence Stitch**

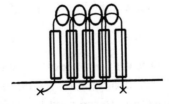

**Fig. 10**
This variation stands upright because the slats of the fence are attached to each other, courtesy of the seed bead.

# Telephone Poles

## Illustration Key:

The -------- line indicates the second pass which adds seed beads to the original stop beads.

**Fig. 11**

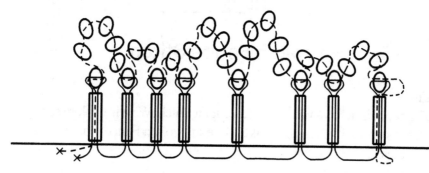

**Fig. 11**

1. Make a scattered series of bugles with a seed bead as a stop bead. These can be made in a straight row, but by spreading and scattering them, an interesting pattern will emerge.

2. Go back up to the right side of the fabric and come out of the *last bugle and stop bead.* Do not put on any beads until out of the stop bead. (This is the beginning of the - - - - line of the graph.)

3. Put more seed beads on your needle than the distance to the next bugle/seed. Go through the seed bead only. Put on more seeds than the distance to the next bugle/seed and continue in this manner. By adding more seeds than the distance between poles, wavy telephone wires and leaning poles are created.

## Corkscrew

**Fig. 12**

Come up to the right side of the fabric and put on 16 seed beads. Any even number will work. The 16th bead (closest to the needle) will be the stop bead. Pass the needle and thread back through the 15th bead.

Continue to pass the needle and thread through every odd bead (13th, 11th, 9th, etc.) until you pass through the 1st bead and through the fabric to the wrong side. Pull thread tension as you go through the beads.

Pull the thread tension tightly. Do you see the corkscrew? Tight tension is a must, so tighten as outlined in the last paragraph of page 40.

**Fig. 12**

**Fig. 13**

## Zig Zag

**Fig. 13**

Start the same as the Corkscrew, but put on 17 beads, or any odd number. After going back through the 16th bead, skip 2 beads, go through two beads. Repeat until you go through the 1st bead and the fabric to the wrong side. Pull tightly, and adjust tension.

● ● ● ● ● ● ● ● ● ● ● ● ● ● ● ● ● ● ● ● ● ●

**Challenges for the Corkscrew and Zig Zag:**
1. Alternate seed bead and larger bead, (size 11, then size 6, etc.)

2. Make a grouping of Corkscrews or Zig Zags or a combination. What image does this texture evoke?

# Sea Weed

## Illustration Key:

The - - - - line is a visual aid to the thread pattern sequence of this stitch.
**Fig. 14**

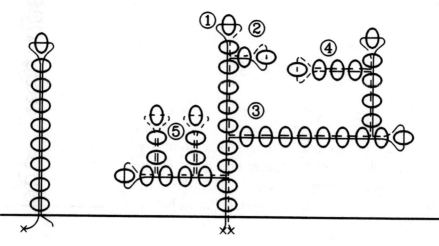

## Fig. 14

This Sea Weed has a "trunk, branches, and twigs." It may not be anatomically correct, but it does give the illusion of sea weed. This is one of the few stitches where a single thread may be needed, depending on the size of the seed bead holes.

Caution: Start with a long thread. Use seed beads with large holes.

The drawing on the left shows what a row of seed beads with one stop bead look likes compared to the Sea Weed Stitch on the right.
To make Sea Weed:

1. On the right side of the fabric, put on a row of 10 seed beads. Using the last bead as a stop bead, go through the second to the last bead with the needle and thread. You have just made the trunk and are at the top of the weed.

2. Your needle and thread should be coming out just under the two top beads in the trunk. You are now ready to make a short branch.

   Put 2 seed beads on the needle and thread, and pull the beads back to the trunk. Use the last bead of the branch as the stop bead. Go back through the remaining bead on this branch with the needle and thread.

   Enter the trunk between the same two beads your thread is coming out of and go down through 4 seed beads of the trunk. Come out at this new point on the trunk. You have just made a branch without twigs.

   Adjust your tension as outlined in the last paragraph on page 40.

47

3. This branch will have two twigs. Put on 9 seed beads to form the branch. After the stop bead, go into only the next bead on the branch and come out. Adjust thread tension.

4. Put on 5 seed beads to make a twig. Put the needle through only the second to the last bead in the twig and come back out to make another twig. Adjust tension. Put on 4 seed beads and put the needle back through all beads except the stop bead. Adjust thread tension. Then, go back through the first twig to the branch, and back through the branch to the trunk. Adjust tension.

5. Start a new branch and twig. Continue until you have a full, fringed sea weed plant.

**Challenges:**
1. Using one or more stitches on this trail, create a funky textural design. Focus on the process, not the product.

2. Create a fantasy plant or animal using a combination of bead appliqué and/or the texture stitches in this chapter.

# Edging and Fringe

Unlike the previous trails, these stitches are worked on the edge or hemline of fabric. They are great for adding finesse to garments, as well as for decoration and home decor projects.

Pocket tops, shirt and dress hems, cuffs, yokes, pillows, table runners, lamp shades, drapery tie-backs, quilts and wall hangings are just a few of the potential applications for fringe and edging stitches.

You will be amazed at the ease of adding sparkle and interest to all your projects with these techniques!

**Before Beading:** READ PREPARATION CHECKLIST page 19.

## Illustration Key:

For edging and fringe stitches, the long horizontal line _____ is the hem or finished edge of the fabric. The illustrations show the edging and fringe hanging down from the finished edge. Typically, edging or fringing is the final step in the project after all other construction has been completed.

Look closely at the illustrations and you will see a small back stitch in the fabric after each sequence is completed. It is the short horizonal line the thread is making above the edge of the fabric. *This back stitch is a stitch from the wrong side of the edge* (where your hem has been sewn) *to the right side of the edge* (the right side of the fabric). Stay close to the edge at all times *piercing the fabric close to the edge.* If you pierce too far up, the fringe/edging and the fabric will not lay flat.

The fringe stitches dangle more and have more movement than the edging stitches. So consider the desired end result when choosing to use edging or fringe.

Challenge yourself! Experiment and try sequences other than those illustrated. If your inner critic surfaces, use a "Bead of Wisdom" to soothe it.

# 3 Bead Scallop Edging

**Fig 1**

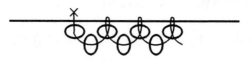

**Fig. 1**

1. After knotting the thread, pierce the hem edge close to the edge, bringing the needle and thread to the right side of the fabric.

2. Put 3 seed beads on the needle, hence the name 3 Bead Scallop Edging. Pierce the hem edge close to the edge *from the wrong side to the right side* approximately 1 bead away from the first bead.

3. Once your needle has pierced the hem edge wrong side to right side, move it directly down through bead 3. With the bulk of the garment upward away from the hem, the needle passes through the hole in bead 3, down and away from the bulk of the fabric.

4. You are now ready to start the next scallop sequence. If you choose to make a uniform scallop edge, put on *2 beads* for each scallop for the remainder of the edging. In this sequence, each new scallop shares 1 bead with the scallop before it.

5. To finish the scallop edge, knot the thread on the wrong side of the hemline.

**Challenges:**
1. **Fig. 2.** Use a larger bead as bead 2 in each sequence

2. Replace beads 1 and 3 with bugle beads.

**Fig. 2.**

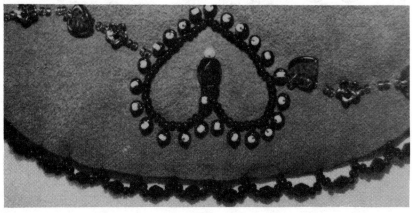

# More Edging Stitches

**Fig. 3**

Key: The term *column* refers to the beads that form the vertical placement of the beads in each sequence.

Vary the size and length of each edging sequence by changing three variables:
1. Number of beads in column.
2. Number of beads in horizontal edge.
3. Size of beads

To keep the edging flat, the placement of the second column is important. It is determined by the length of the beads in the horizontal edge. Example: If there are 4 beads in the horizontal edge, place the second column and all future columns 4 bead lengths from the preceding column in the sequence.

**Challenges:**
1. **Fig. 3.** Experiment with the 6 illustrated sequences.

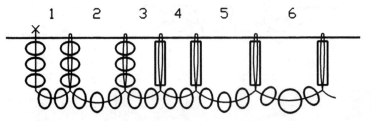

2. Create a pattern by alternating between two of the six illustrated sequences.

3. Invent new sequences.

4. To make the edging wave, put on more horizontal edge beads than the distance between the columns.

# Fringe

**Before beading:** READ PREPARATION CHECKLIST page 19.

**Fig. 4**

Fringe is a fluid form of edging. Because it is more fluid, it is necessary to consider the wear and tear factor of the fringe. It can be easily caught on other objects. Therefore, it is highly recommended that a *knot* be made on the wrong side of the fabric *after completing each sequence.* If the fringe does catch and break a thread, it is much easier to repair one sequence than numerous or all sequences. "A stitch in time, saves nine."

Another fringe consideration is thread tension. Loose tension will cause thread to show, and the sequences will not look uniform. Tight tension fringe will not be fluid and will curl up. To review tension control, see the last paragraph of Stop Stitch page 40.

**Fig. 4**

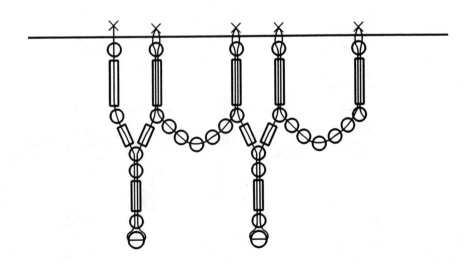

**Fig 4** (continued)

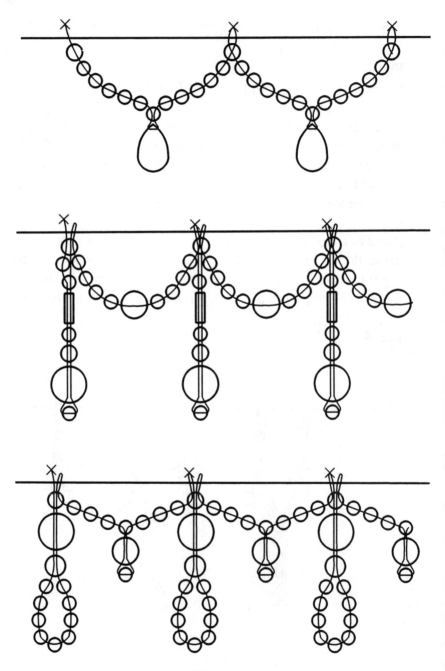

The fringe sequences in **Fig. 4** are worked from left to right. By following the illustrated thread lines and taking the small back stitches through the fold with the thread wrong side to right side as indicated, you can complete a row of any of these joined fringe examples in one pass.

**Challenges:**

1. Invent and combine new fringe sequences.

2. Are there stitches in Trail 7, "Creating Texture With Beads," that can be adapted to fringe sequences?

# Brick Stitch Edging

The Brick or Comanche Stitch can be worked on fabric as a surface embellishment, or on a hemline or finished edge. You may be familiar with the Brick Stitch as the triangle top of the fringed Native American style earrings. As a fabric edging, individual bead triangles may be beaded. Or, make a series of triangles that share a common base.

# Individual Triangles

**Fig 5**
Using the following edging technique, make a group of five 2 bead edging as illustrated on the left of **Fig 5**, a total of 6 beads.

1. Knot the thread the bring the needle up to the right side of fabric.

2. Put on 2 beads, pierce the edge of the fabric from the wrong side to the right side and go back down through the 2nd bead.3. Put on bead 3, pierce the fabric wrong side to the right side, and go back down through bead 3.

4. Repeat for beads 4, 5, and 6.

5. After going back down through bead 6, put on bead 7 to start row 2.

6. Guide the needle and thread *over the thread* connecting bead 5 and 6 *from behind forward*. Then pass the needle down through bead 7.

7. Put on bead 8 amd repeat #6 across the second row.

8. Continue with each row adding 1 less bead until the last row which has only 1 bead.

**Fig. 5**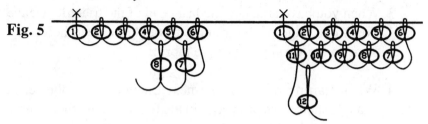

9. After putting on the last bead at the point of the triangle, go over the thread and back down through this last bead as you have done with all other beads.

10. See the left triangle in **Fig. 6**. Weave the needle and thread through the end bead's hole in each row on one side of the triangle until you reach the fabric. Pierce the fabric to the wrong side and knot.

**Fig. 6**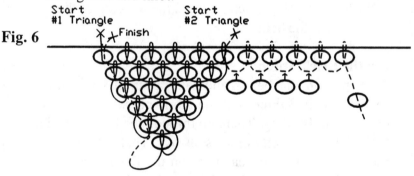

# Joined Triangles

1. In the first row, joined edging triangles share a common bead with the triangles on either side. Start by sewing on the base row for only the first triangle using the 2 bead edging stitch. For the first and last triangle, you will be sewing on 6 base beads. For the middle triangles, sew on 5 base beads. Only two triangles are illustrated in **Fig. 6**.

2. Work all remaining rows as in **Fig. 6**. You will bead all rows of each individual triangle, *one triangle at a time.*

3. When you have attached the last bead of the triangle, weave down one edge of the triangle through the bead holes and knot on the wrong side of the fabric.

4. When starting row 1 of the next triangle, remember each triangle shares one base bead in the first row with the triangle on either side of it. **Fig. 6**

### Challenges:

1. Any edging stitch, including the Brick Stitch, can be worked on a flat fabric surface. Instead of piercing the edge of the hem, pierce the flat fabric down and back up to the right side in a small sewing stitch. This small sewing stitch replaces the piercing of the fold line of the hem.

### For the Brick Stitch:

First, put on the beads and take a small stitch under approximately 3 threads of the fabric perpendicular to the row you are beading. Then, go through the bead butted up to the fabric a second time as always. This will produce a ridge of dimensional beadwork on the flat surface of the fabric. Visualize "The Great Wall of China" as you make an edging stitch sequence across the flat fabric.

2. When constructing a beaded ridge, (or wall) on a flat fabric surface, draw a gentle wavy line on your fabric first. Then, follow the line constructing your base row for the edging stitch on the line as #1 above.

**Challenges (cont'd):**

3. Graph a Brick Stitch pattern and work it into the brick stitch triangles as you contruct them.

4. Work edging or fringe on the edge of twill tape which is taped to cardboard. Sew finished piece to a lampshade or use glue that will not deteriorate near heat.

**Bracelet Of Life**
Kelly Johnson
*Back Stitch, Lazy Stitch, Couching*

# Crazy Beading

## Converting Embroidery Stitches
## to Bead Patterns

Making Crazy Quilts was all the rage in Victorian times. Crazy Quilts combined embroidery, sewing, appliqué, lace, ribbon, buttons, beading and painting on hand stitched quilts. Animals, birds, insects, children, flowers and Japanese motifs were favorite Victorian subjects. The more intricate and busy they were, the better!

Crazy Quilts were not intended to be practical or used on a bed. They were usually draped over furniture in the parlor. In a chilly parlor, they may have covered a lap while entertaining.

Silk, satin, and velvet scraps were the fabrics of choice for these quilts. Unfortunately, these delicate fabrics held together with detailed embroidered patterns, did not age well. A Victorian Crazy Quilt in good condition is truly a rare find.

Crazy Beading is not limited to seam embellishment on quilt pieces. These stitches work great on yokes, table runners, lapels and anything you can think of!

This trail will teach you how to emulate Victorian Crazy Quilt embroidery patterns with seed beads. Experienced embroiderers will need to focus on new needle placements and techniques to get the embroidery look with seed beads. If you have little or no experience with embroidery stitches, you will not be at a disadvantage.

If you know how to embroider, the good news is: You can change colors without rethreading the needle! However, you will need to learn to hold the beads in place with your fingers until they are secure. Embroidery floss or thread will cling to fabric, beads won't.

In the Appendix, you will find two piecing techniques to construct Crazy Quilts. On the following pages, we will concentrate on the stitch techniques.

*Embellished Chevron*

*Embellished Fans (left), Cretan (center), Three Wide Feather (right)*

*Floral Pattern*

• • • • • • • • • • • • • • • • • • • • • • • •

**Before beading:** READ PREPARATION CHECKLIST page 19.

## Illustration Key:

All views are aerial views. The lines indicate the position of size 11 beads as they lay on the fabric. Individual seed bead positions are not illustrated because the number of beads you use will depend on the shape and size of each bead. Size 14 beads will give you smoother lines, greater detail, and a more delicate look. Reduce the patterns on a copy machine to the size you desire when using size 14 beads.

Use size 11 and size 8 seed beads. The number of beads you use to construct these patterns can vary. Not all size 11 beads are the same size or shape. Choose rounder beads, as opposed to squarer beads, for a smoother look.

The ends of the illustrated lines are where the lines of beads will end and where the needle and thread pierce the fabric and pass down to the wrong side of the fabric.

Thread tension can make a big difference in the finished Crazy Beading pattern. The use of a hoop or canvas stretcher will aid in keeping the fabric flat.

Let's get started!

# Patterns

1. Lay a piece of transparent, stiff plastic over the patterns in this book. This will prevent your felt tip marker from going through the tissue paper and onto your master pattern. A single sheet of a plastic page protector for a 3 ring binder is cheap and works fine!

2. Lay the plastic sheet over the pattern, and lay a sheet of tissue paper on top of the plastic.

3. Trace the pattern with a fine tip marker onto the tissue paper. If you need a pattern that is longer than the master pattern, move down the book, connect and trace another section.

   Use only one tissue paper pattern at a time. When you have several tissue patterns pinned to the fabric at once it can be difficult beading. The pins will catch on the working thread and the tissue can tear.

4. Pin the tissue paper pattern securely to your fabric with numerous pins.

5. Bead through the tissue paper pattern and the fabric for each of the Crazy Beading patterns. Tear away the tissue paper when you finish beading. The tissue paper tears away best in dry conditions. Tweezers work well to remove any tiny paper pieces.

# Fans

## Illustration Key:

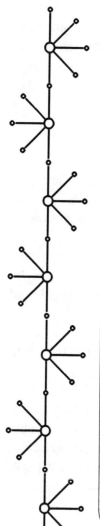

Straight lines are bugles. Circles are size 8 seed beads with size 11 stop beads. Small dots indicate 1 seed bead with a stop bead.

1. Sew a size 8 bead with a stop bead to each circle.

2. Sew on bugles radiating out from the size 8's, one fan at a time.

3. At the outer end of each bugle, sew 1 seed bead with 1 stop bead.

**Challenges:**

1. Substitute all 11's with 8's using an 11 as a stop bead. (Each fan must now share an 8 with a neighboring fan.)

2. After securing 8's with an 11 stop bead, run a curved line of 11's through all stop beads on the fan edges. This outlines and connects all fans in a repeating "S" pattern.

# Chevron Stitch

## Illustration Key:

All beads are size 11 seed beads. Use the Lazy Stitch to:

1. Work down the fabric, beading all short parallel lines of beads.

2. Connect the center of the parallel rows with two 45 degree angle rows of seed beads. See illustration.

**Challenges:**
1. Choose an embellishment sequence on page 75 and add it to each chevron.

2. Embellish chevrons with a repeating row of fresh water pearls, buttons, shells, etc.

3. Replace some or all rows with bugle beads.

4. Make double bead rows of parallel and/or 45 degree angle rows.

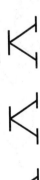

# Two Wide Feather Stitch

## Illustration Key:

All beads are size 11 seed beads.

*Beads cross beads* at the bottom of each "U," not just the thread.

1. Work from top to bottom. Start each "U" from the inside midpoint of each preceding "U."

2. *The first "U" will have a few less beads in it than the rest as it does not overlap a "U."* Start the first "U" by putting on enough beads to form the "U" and go down to the wrong side of fabric.

3. Bring the needle up to the right side of the fabric above and in slightly at the bottom inside curve of the first "U."

4. Put on enough beads to form the second "U." Pull gently to form a rounded "V" from the first "U." Bring the needle down to the wrong side of the fabric following your tissue pattern for the second "U."

5. Repeat #3 and #4. The last rounded "V" is anchored by 3 seed beads.

**Challenges:**

1. On the outer points of the feathers, embellish with options on page 75.

2. Mix and match embellishments:

Use one embellishment on the right outer points of the pattern, and a different embellishment on the left outer points of the pattern.

Vary the colors of the embellishment. Example: Red on right, blue on left.

# Three Wide Feather Stitch

## Illustration Key:

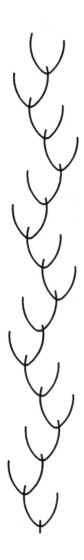

All beads are size 11 seed beads.

1. Work from the top to the bottom the same as for the Two Wide Feather Stitch.

2. After the first feather, there are 3 feathers that angle down to the right then two that angle to the left, etc.

Remember: The completed feathers are slightly rounded "V's."

**Challenges:**
1. Invent new embellishment options for the Feather Stitch.

2. Change the color of every feather.

# Cretan Stitch

## Illustration Key:

All beads are size 11.

*Beads cross beads* at each "X" intersection.

1. Stitch 1 complete distorted "X" at a time as indicated by the numbering on the illustration.

2. Put on approximately 2 more beads than can lay in a straight line from #1 to #2.

3. Each stitch, after the beginning stitch, will pull and make a *bend at the crossing point* of the preceding stitch. If you have the right number of beads and good tension, the beads will be tight to the fabric and look like the pattern on this page.

> **Challenge:**
> 1. Embellishments can go at any point of the stitch, or on the fabric inside the "V" area. Experiment and discover!

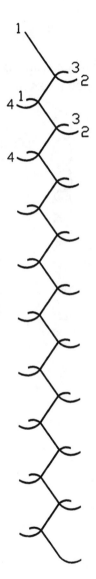

# Chain Stitch

## Illustration Key:

All beads are size 11 seed beads. The graph shows what the finished stitch looks like.

1. Work from the top to the bottom. You do not need to use a tissue paper pattern as long as your beads are uniform in size and you use the same number of beads per chain.

2. Put on enough seed beads to make the desired size link. Make sure an odd number is used such as seven or nine. Put the needle back through the top of the hole in the first bead you put on and pass it down through the fabric to the wrong side, completing a link.

3. Come up in approximately the middle of the preceding link. Put on the same number of seed beads and repeat as #2 above. End with 2 or 3 beads as shown. This is a bulky stitch.

**Challenges:**
1. Curve the chain.     2. Layer chains.

# Floral Patterns

## Illustration Key:

Size 11 seed beads and size 8 beads with 11's for stop beads.

1. Sew the curved lines first with the Back Stitch as on Trail 6.

2. One flower at a time, put on size 8's with a seed bead as a stop bead.

3. Work the petals of the flower with 1 link of the Chain Stitch. Come up near the center of the petal and anchor the petal with 3 beads over the rounded petal edge.

4. Knot and start the next flower.

**Challenges:**
1. Create a floral pattern on a vine from the next page.

2. Add grapes as on page 75 to the vines in the place of flowers.

3. Add embellishment options as on page 75.

4. Invent new embellishment combinations.

# Vine Variations

# Embellishment Variations

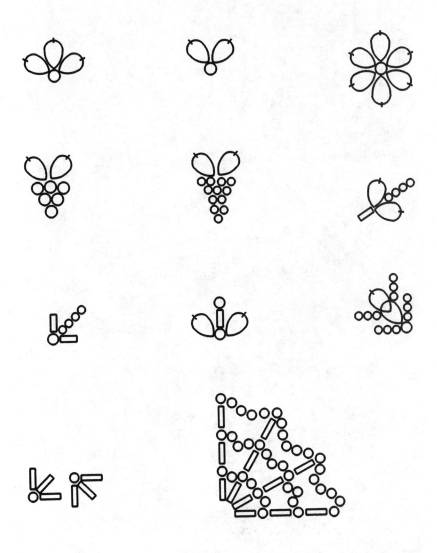

**All Things Old Are New Again**
Nancy Eha
*Back Stitch, Crazy Beading, Beaded Counted Canvas, Beaded Trapunto, Beaded Quilting, Edging Stitch*

Thank you for your purchase of my book, Off The Beadin' Path. I hope it will guide and inspire you to discover your own creative trail of bead embellishment.

I am currently scheduling lectures and workshops for the second half of 1998 and beyond. If you know of a guild, society, shop, or organization who may be interested, please have them contact me c/o Creative Visions Press. The address and phone number can be found on the page opposite "About The Author" at the front of this book.

Dare To Be Creative,

Nancy

# Changing Fabric Surfaces

On this trail, beaded needleworking techniques which give height and depth to fabric surfaces will be explored. Beaded Quilting, Beaded Trapunto, and Beaded Coils are easy to master and provide spectacular results.

Think of other sewing or needlework techniques you already know. How can you adapt them to beading? Now, go for it!

The embroidery Back Stitch can be transformed in beads as shown on Trail 6. If you have preprinted detailed embroidery patterns to bead the Back Stitch on, use size 14 seed beads. You could also enlarge the pattern on a copy machine and use size 11 seed beads.

## Hand Quilting with Beads

A quilt consists of 3 layers: top fabric, batting, and back fabric. By adding beads with hand stitching, depth and contrast are added to

● ● ● ● ● ● ● ● ● ● ● ● ● ● ● ● ● ● ● ● ● ● ● ●

the fabric surface. Beaded quilting will achieve the greatest contrast on a solid colored fabric as opposed to a patterned fabric.

Proportion is a consideration when using quilting patterns. The beads take up more space than quilting thread. Choose larger, less detailed patterns for beading or consider using size 14 beads.
The stitch used for beaded quilting is the Running Stitch. The running stitch moves in a continuous forward pattern. It produces a broken line of beads on the right side of the fabric and a line of small stitches on the wrong side of the fabric. Both the right side (with beads) and the back side (with thread) will look like this: _ _ _ _ _ _ _ _ _

Aim for approximately 8 stitches per inch (4 on the right side and 4 on the back side). Each time your needle comes up to the right side of the fabric, put on 1-2 beads and go down through to the back side.

Ideas for patterns include: quilting templates, stencil patterns, embroidery patterns using the running stitch, and white-work patterns.

**Before beading:** READ PREPARATION CHECKLIST page 19.

1. Draw the pattern on the right side of fabric with a quilting pencil or by the tissue paper method used for Crazy Beading. Another option would be to trace larger, less complex patterns on tear away Pellon.

2. Baste the three layers together. Your long stitches will be in rows at two inch intervals. Baste from the center outward both vertically and horizontally. Next, baste around the perimeter. If you are making a quilt, sew the binding on at this time. The Pellon or tissue paper pattern will be pinned or basted as the fourth and top layer.

3. Fit the layers taut in a quilt frame, hoop, or canvas stretcher. (See page 26). You may not need to use a stretching device if you use good thread tension. A hoop works best for small areas. Start in the center and bead quilt the main lines first. Then, go back and work the details. Work from the center out for best control.

4. Remove your work from the frame. If you are making something other than a quilt, construct the project. Lastly, take out the basting stitches.

## Beaded Running Stitch Variations

The following quilting patterns can be worked as beaded quilting stitches using the Running Stitch. Before beading: READ PREPARATION CHECKLIST page 19.

## Vermicelli

**Fig. 1**

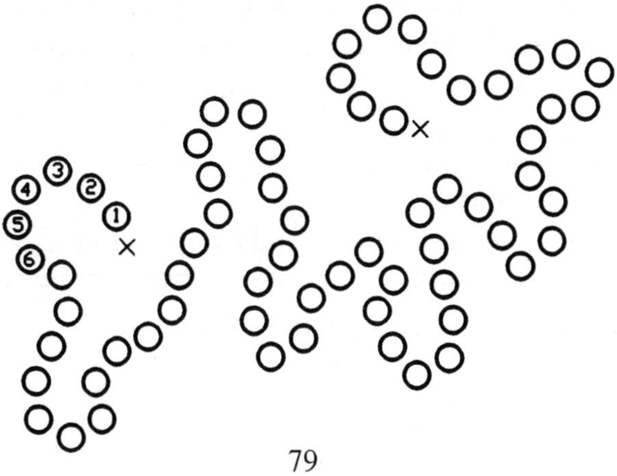

79

## Fig. 1

Draw a meandering, continuous line on tissue paper. The line will be your pattern guide. Do not draw directly on the fabric for this stitch. You will be following the line, sewing on a bead, skipping a bead's space, sewing on another bead, and so on. Size 14 seed beads work best for this stitch. Size 11 gives the work a coarser look.

# Broken Noodles

## Fig. 2

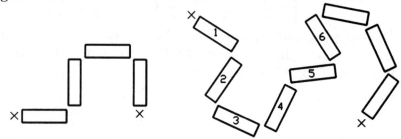

## Fig.2

Just go for this one and do not draw a pattern. Each bugle is sewn on independently. Broken noodles are most interesting if the degree of the angle of the bugle beads is continually changed.

**Challenge:**
1. Combine Vermicelli and Broken Noodles.

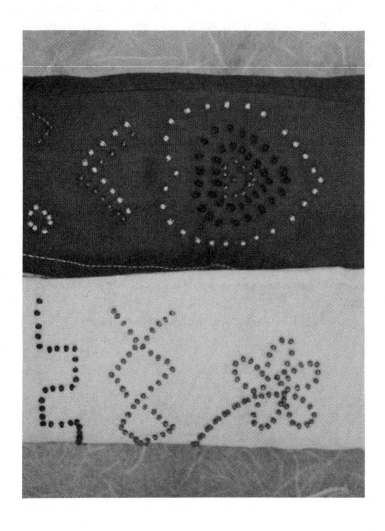

# Quilting Patterns

Quilting patterns will be more apparent on solid color fabrics. A pattern can be marked on the fabric, drawn on tissue paper or tear away Pellon, and basted into place. Templates can be made of cardboard and traced on the fabric with a quilters pencil. Experiment with bead and pattern size, *before starting* on a project. Lines of quilting can be 1/2" or greater apart. Beaded quilting can cover a specific area or the entire fabric surface.

## Cross Hatching

**Fig. 3**

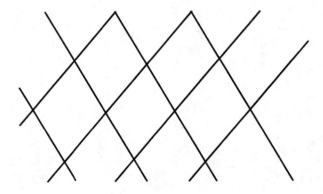

**Fig. 3**
Masking tape can be used as a template on the fabric. The quilting is done along the edges of the tape. Do not leave tape on longer than 8 hours, and do not use tape on Ultra Suede, velvet or any fabric with a nap.

## Pumpkin Seeds

**Fig. 4**

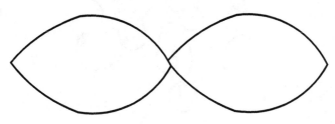

## Clam Shell

**Fig. 5**

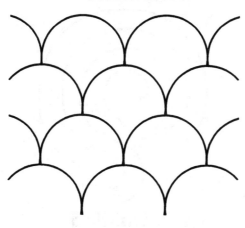

## Square Stipple

**Fig. 6**

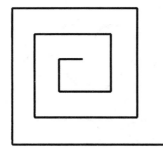

## Meandering Stipple

**Fig. 7**

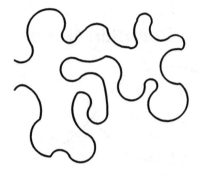

## Finger Print

**Fig. 8**

## Echo Quilting

**Fig. 9**

**Fig. 9**

The lines are quite close on this pattern for size 11 seed beads. You may either enlarge it on a copy machine or remove some of the echo lines. Experiment before starting your projects.

**Challenge:**

1. Cut snowflakes, hearts or other "paper doll" type of patterns for bead quilting templates. Glue the paper pattern to light weight cardboard using a glue stick. Cut out the cardboard template.

# Beaded Trapunto

Trapunto is the stitching of shapes with tight close Back Stitches through two layers of fabric. The bottom layer is then slit open from the back side and stuffed with batting until the top layer pops firmly out. The slit is then sewn shut by sewing stitches across the slit to close it.

**Fig. 10**
To create Beaded Trapunto, the back stitches that outline the pattern are sewn with beaded back stitches. Trapunto can be used on patterned fabric to outline flowers, birds, etc. It can also be worked on solid fabric to form it's own beaded pattern.

**Before beading:** READ PREPARATION CHECKLIST page 19.

**Fig. 10**

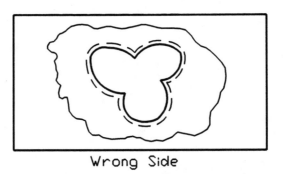

Wrong Side

1. If using solid fabric, draw the pattern on muslin. This will be the bottom layer. Pin the muslin to the *wrong* side of the fabric in the area(s) you want to work. If outlining an area of patterned fabric, you will follow the pattern. No need to draw on the muslin.

2. Outline the pattern through both layers of fabric, with a *tight* running stitch using a high contrast color of thread.

3. Carefully cut a 1" slit in the muslin with the points of a small scissors. Stuff firmly with polyester batting, but not to the point of puckering. Close the muslin slit by sewing it shut with small overhand stitches.

4. On the right side of the fabric, sew a beaded back stitch through all layers of fabric just inside the shape on the running stitch line. Remove the running stitch.

**Challenges:**

1. Cover the raised areas of your Trapunto design with the Lazy Stitch. Pull the thread tight in every row to keep the beads secure.

2. Cover the design area with a bead stitch such as the Stop Stitch or the Dangle Stop Stitch on the top fabric only. Then make the small beaded stitches around the shape, slit, and stuff. What happened?

3. Use a tight knit fabric such as Spandex or Lycra for the top fabric of the Trapunto. By stuffing tightly, you achieve a higher dimension than with woven fabrics.

4. Combine Beaded Trapunto with Beaded Quilting.

# Beaded Coils

Beaded coils are round cords with the lazy stitch worked over the cording. The hat I am wearing on the front cover, "Jackie O. Lunches With Timothy Leary," is embellished with beaded coils. This cording can be found in either the trim, upholstery or drapery tie-back sections of a fabric store. Look for cord with a smooth surface. It is a bonus if the cords are colored. A portion of the cord can be left unbeaded and will add additional color and texture to your art. I used 1/4" cord for the hat on this book's cover.

This is a process that must be used with a fabric stretching device because the stitches on the wrong side of the fabric are long and tight. This combination will develop wrinkles on the fabric where you don't want them!

A design consideration of Beaded Coils is that the finished coil will not let your fabric drape. Do not use this process on any project that needs to be fluid. Beaded Coils can be used on pillows, lapels, purses, hats and other projects where you want the fabric to keep its form.

• • • • • • • • • • • • • • • • • • • • • • • • • •

**Before beading:** READ PREPARATION CHECKLIST page 19.

### Fig. 11 and 12

1. Baste the fabric to muslin and insert in to a hoop or canvas stretcher.

2. Baste cording in position on the right side of fabric, on top of the fabric and muslin.

3. Knot the thread and pass the needle up to the right side of the fabric where the cord sides meet the fabric.

4. Put on enough beads to cover the diameter of the coil.

5. Lay the row of beads over the hump of the coil, and take the needle and thread down to the wrong side of the fabric close to the cord edge using the Lazy Stitch. See Trail 6 for Lazy Stitch directions.

6. **Fig 11.** Bring thread across the wrong side of fabric and up to the right side next to the 1st row of beads. Continue beading over the cord in this manner.

### Fig. 11

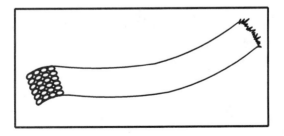

7. The ends of the cord will fray. The fraying may be left exposed, or bind it back into the shape and bead over it.

8. **Fig 12**. When beading over a curve of a coil, sew two rows from the inner-most point outward. Then, go back and fill in the open area with partial rows.

**Fig. 12**

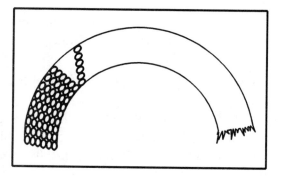

**Challenges:**

1. Change bead colors to make stripes or a dot pattern.

2. Leave some cord showing.

3. After covering the cord with the Lazy Stitch, go back and add dangles, fringe, etc. on the surface of the beaded coil.

# Sculpting Fabric Shapes

There may be times when you want your three dimensional beaded fabric pieces to be provided with a support system to hold a desired shape. Beads can add more weight than the fabric alone can support. Therefore, an invisible support system needs to be constructed. This will prevent your art piece from caving in on itself.

## Hidden Wire Support

Sandwiching wire between two layers of fabric (beaded and a lining) will allow you to bend, twist and put your art into numerous configurations.

Wire is available in many gauges (sizes) at hardware stores. You will be able to find the thinner gauges in bead shops. Pick a gauge that is thin enough to be hidden and strong enough to support the shape of your art. You can get away with hiding a thick, 16 gauge galvanized steel wire in a peyote tube, but it is too bulky to be hidden between two pieces of fabric.

If you are hiding the wire between fabric, you need to use a thinner gauge such as 20 or 24 gauge. These gauges are available in larger bead shops. For larger or heavier projects, chose 20-24 galvanized steel wire found at hardware stores. Although the gauges are the same, the galvanized steel is firmer and it will hold its shape better if weight is an issue.

It is important to use galvanized or copper wires to avoid rusting. If in doubt regarding a specific wire, ask a hardware store employee.

Ultra suede is my fabric of choice for sculpted beaded fabric surfaces. It comes in many colors and is not a suede or animal product. Ultra Suede is a man-made material. Ultra Suede has the look and feel of suede, but is easier to sew through and it can be machine washed and dried. You can find 9" squares for sale in a multitude of colors at Minnesota or Hancock Fabrics for around $3.00. In the fall, it may be available on a bolt, but be prepared to pay $60.00 a yard. For small projects, look for the squares. Mail order sources are included in the Appendix.

The most beneficial feature of Ultra Suede is that there is no raveling of the cut edges. No need to seam, turn under, or hide raw edges. I am for anything that makes my life simpler!

# 7 Step Sandwich Process

1. For the front and back sides, draw the pattern cutting edge on the Ultra Suede twice using a pen or pencil. You will make a sandwich. The Ultra Suede is the bread and the rubber cement and wire are the meat and cheese. Remember to make the pattern for the back in reverse by turning over the pattern piece before drawing around it.

2. Paint, embroider, and/or surface bead one or both right sides. If beading, adjust your thread tension so that the fabric lays flat. Leave at least a 1/4" fabric boarder from your beading to the drawn pattern edge.

3. Cut out both pieces on the inner edge of your pen markings so that the ink is not on your cut out piece.

4. Cut a length of 20 gauge wire long enough to follow the outer perimeter of one piece.

5. **Fig. 1.** Shape the wire to fit inside the inner edge of one piece. The wire form is a rough shape and it does not need to follow the shape of every little wave or corner of the fabric. With pointed pieces such as the daisy in the following section, a piece of straight wire down the middle will work.

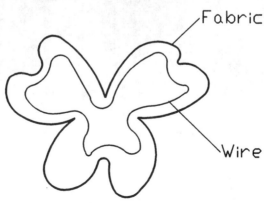

**Fig 1**

Fabric

Wire

6. Lift the wire up and apply a thin coat of rubber cement to both wrong sides of the Ultra Suede.

7. Lay the wire on the wrong side of one piece, put the other piece on top, wrong sides together. Smooth out and let dry for a minimum of one hour. Next, bend and experiment with the piece to find your desired shape. There are many right answers!

If the rubber cement is showing, you can easily rub it off with your finger when it is dry. Rubber cement will not stain the Ultra Suede.

# Ultra Suede Flowers

**Fig. 2**

Following are patterns for: Daisy or Day Lily, Wild Rose, Leaf, and Wood Violet (2 pieces). The Daisy or Day Lily is determined by the direction you bend and form the petals. The Day Lily has a greater curve to the petal. By hand sewing or glue gun, attach them to your projects. They are fun on hats, pins, photo frames, etc.

Construct the flowers using the preceding 7 Step Sandwich Process. Then, before bending, finish off all edges with a 3 Bead Scallop Edging Stitch. See Trail 8. Size 14 beads work best for the Wood Violet or other smaller patterns, size 11 beads for larger pieces. The Wood Violet is constructed in two parts then sewn together using beads to hide the stitches in the flower's center.

Use tracing or tissue paper to trace these patterns.

**Fig. 2**

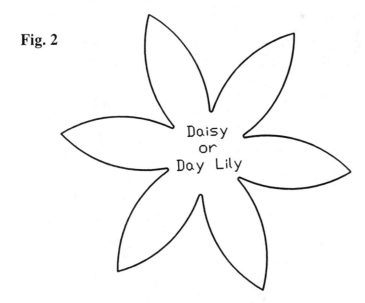

**Fig. 2** (cont'd)

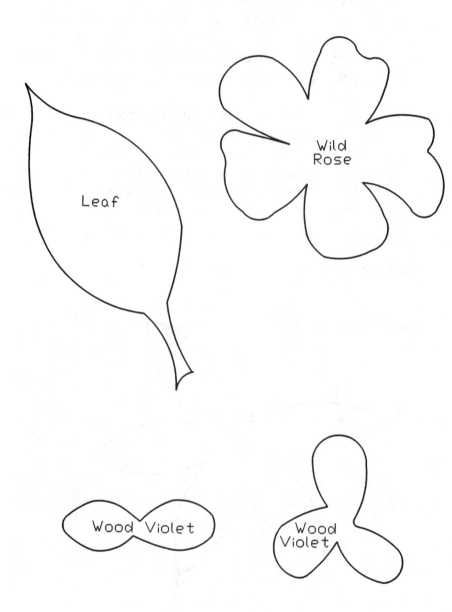

**Challenges:**

1. Experiment with shapes other than flowers. Animals, insects and sea creatures have potential.

2. Construct long strips, ripple and make into a mobile.

3. Construct shapes, then attach to small peyote stitch or loomwork pieces to form vessels, sculpture, etc.

4. Trap your ideas! Sketch your ideas in your Idea Keeper section of your Discovery Journal.

**Honoring Fertility** (Vessel)
Nancy Eha
*Bead Embellished Fabric With Hidden Wire Support,*
*Peyote Stitch Variations*

# PVC Plastic

PVC plastic sheets are thin flexible sheets. When heated they can be bent and when cooled, they retain the new bent shape. PVC holds it's shape better, and can sustain more weight than wire supports. Through much investigating, I found that PVC is used for the thinner credit cards such as library cards and membership cards. If it is not flexible, such as major credit cards, it will not work.

Some plastic sheets used for stenciling work as well. The plastic sheets quilters use to make quilting templates may also work. See Appendix.

The thinner versions of PVC, stenciling and quilting templates, will bend under the weight of a heavily beaded fabric. If you will be sewing dense beading on your fabric surface, layer two or three sheets of the thin PVC together. After cutting duplicate shapes from the sheets, adhere the layers together with rubber cement or sew through all layers on the perimeter of the shape with a sewing machine.

The thicker the PVC, the more weight of a bead embellished fabric it can hold and still keep it's shape. My best source for the thicker sheets is a surplus store where I bought two foot square sheets that have a cougar print on them. (Who knows why?) So check your local surplus sources. Check also with your health club, library, etc. and ask where they buy their cards. Look in the yellow pages for plastic card companies and see if they will sell you scraps, misprints, etc. It does not matter what color the PVC is as it will be a hidden support system.

Once you find a source, verify it is PVC by testing a scrap. **Warning: PVC when heated or melted does emit toxic fumes. Work in a large well-ventilated area.** Turn a hand held blow dryer on hot and hold it 3 inches from the PVC. Use gloves to protect your hands from the heat. Blow on both sides of the sheet and within seconds, you should be able to quickly bend the PVC into a new shape.

You do need to work quickly, so it is helpful to have both hands free to do the bending. Use a vise to hold the blow dryer in place, or use the buddy system. Have a friend hold the blow dryer and both your hands will be free to manipulate the PVC.

Between the blow dryer method and the following boiling water method, I prefer the blow dryer method for safety reasons. You do run the risk of burning yourself with boiling water. You can bend and control smaller specific areas of the PVC with a blow dryer. Also, you do not have to wait for the wet Ultra Suede to dry.

To bend small pieces you may try boiling water in a pot that you will not use for food in the future. Use <u>heavy</u> rubber gloves without holes and tongs to drop the PVC in or dip a PVC scrap. Take every precaution not to burn yourself with the boiling water. The PVC instantaneously becomes flexible. Remove it with the tongs and bend with your rubber gloved hands.

I use a PVC process similar to the preceding wire 7 Step Sandwich Method. You can follow the same directions on pages 93-94, with these exceptions:

1. Draw a pattern on the piece(s) of PVC. Trim the PVC pattern approximately 1/4" smaller on all edges than your fabric sandwich pieces will be. If you do not trim the PVC, that is fine. However, you will not be able to do an edging stitch around the edges.

2. and 3. Same

4. and 5. Ignore all.

6. Do not use wire. Replace the wire with the PVC piece and glue with rubber cement.

7. After the rubber cement is dry, use the blow dryer method to shape.

For large heavily bead encrusted surfaces, you may need to make hidden sewing stitches to help maintain the new shape. Caution: Large numbers of bugle beads, sewn flat on the fabric, may not allow pieces to curve. It is advisable to test your theories on a small scale before you start a project.

**Challenges:**

1. Experiment with different bead formations and shaping PVC.

2. Join beaded PVC shapes together with other beads to make collages, wall sculpture, earrings, or necklaces.

# Milk Bottle Plastic

Wash out your empty milk bottles. They are not made of PVC, but make a great flat support base for Ultra Suede broaches, earrings, pennants, picture frames, and other projects you will invent.

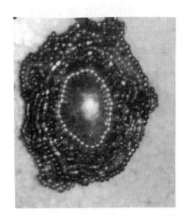

*Pendant: Couching on fabric with plastic bottle support as directions on this page*

1. Create a template of the desired shape out of light weight cardboard such as a file card.

2. Trace the template on a flat surface of the clean milk bottle, and cut out the shape.

3. Lay the milk bottle template on Ultra Suede and trace around it making an Ultra Suede pattern approximately 1/4" larger on all edges than the milk bottle piece.

4. Bead embellish the Ultra Suede surface leaving 1/4" area on all sides. Monitor your thread tension so the fabric continues to lay flat.

5. Cut out the Ultra Suede piece on the line you drew.

6. Apply a thin coat of rubber cement evenly on the milk bottle plastic and glue it to the wrong side of the fabric. Let dry for at least five minutes. If the fabric did not adhere, apply more rubber cement.

7. Pull the unbeaded edges of the Ultra Suede around to the back side of the plastic, and secure it with rubber cement. The Ultra Suede will allow some stretching. If needed, clip the excess ridges of fabric off the back side.

8. Using the template, cut another piece of Ultra Suede to the *template size*. Apply rubber cement to this fabric piece and press it down over the back side of the plastic and the folded Ultra Suede egde.Trim if needed. If the rubber cement leaks out, you can rub it off when it is dry.

9. You may need to stitch small overhand stitches around the back side to hold the two pieces of Ultra Suede together.

**Challenges:**
1. Use a pre-cut mat board with an oval cutout of the center as a picture frame template and follow the preceding directions. You will need to clip the folded edges of Ultra Suede on the backside of the oval to allow the material to "fan out" and lay flat. Plan ahead to be sure your piece of Ultra Suede is large enough. If not:

A. Machine sew pieces together, and clip the seam allowance back. Let the wrong side with seam allowande showing be the right side of the fabric to give it a "ridged" look.

**Challenges (cont')**
B. Use the Fusible Webbing: No Sew Method for Crazy
    Quilt Patchwork in the Appendix to make a larger
    piece of Ultra Suede from scraps.

**Button Forms Covered With
Bead Appliqué**
Carol Berry (left), Robin Atkins (top and right)

**Spring Death**
Deborah Sproule
*Lazy Stitch*

# Beading On
# Counted Canvas

Needlepoint canvas was often used in the construction of antique beaded purses. Our beading foremothers used needlepoint canvas known as Penelope cloth. It was not as heavy as the needlepoint canvas known today as Penelope cloth.

On vintage beaded bags, beads were sewn on the canvas in many ways. One of the popular ways was with a regular needlepoint stitch in which the beads were put on the canvas diagonally. Another popular method was with a straight vertical stitch which gives the appearance of loomwork. I will give you directions for the diagonal method. With experimentation, you can adapt the directions for the faux loomwork.

With today's Aida, Penelope, or plastic punched canvas, size 11 beads will be used on 14 count cloth. For size 14 beads, 18 count cloth is needed. You will need to experiment with the fabric you purchase to determine which beads will fit best into the space allotted. There can be much difference in size and shapes of size 11, or any size beads. I have found the round shaped and slightly smallish beads of uniform size work the best. Not all seed beads are round. Most silver lined are not rounded at the holes, but are more tubular shaped. Buy your choice of canvas, experiment with the beads you have, and then shop for your project beads.

# Aida Cloth

Aida cloth can be purchased in many colors at needlework shops. Aida cloth can also be found at craft or fabric stores in limited colors. You may also find hand towels, bibs, etc., with Aida cloth woven into the piece. Narrow bands of Aida cloth are sold as trim to sew onto garments, home decor, etc.

Aida cloth is most often used for counted cross stitch and has a tiny hole in each stitch corner for the needle to pass through. As in cross stitch or needlepoint, you may choose to have fabric showing around your design. The color of the cloth would therefore be a consideration when designing your project.

You will be working from corner to opposite corner of the woven square pattern in the fabric. The corners are indicated by the small holes at each corner. The seed bead will rest on the interior fabric of each of the woven squares.

On large pieces, work with a large hoop or canvas stretcher. Small pieces can be hand held, but you will need to bind the edges by basting under the raw edges or machine stitching near the edges with a narrow zigzag. This will keep the edges from fraying and the fabric grid from shifting.

# Penelope Cloth

Penelope cloth holds it's shape better than Aida and the holes are much bigger than Aida. The holes are so large that Penelope cloth resembles window screen. Penelope cloth is made for use with wool yarn for needlepoint. It is sold only in dark beige and white. Due to the limited color selection and large holes, I prefer to cover the entire surface with a bead design. No matter what the shape of your finished design, you can finish off the raw edges. Fold the edges back to the wrong side of the canvas and sew them in place.

To keep the ends from catching on your working thread, baste under the raw edges of the canvas. You have the option of buying your canvas blank and charting yourself or pre-painted patterns for needlepoint are available at needlework shops and work for beading as well.

# Plastic Punched Paper

This is the plastic version of punched paper which is used in Victorian crafts. This is the easiest counted canvas to use. The holes are large, the raw edges do not need to be taped, and the canvas will not shift.

This plastic material will not drape and the raw edges cannot be folded under as with Aida or Penelope cloth. However, if you are careful not to cut a beading thread, the excess plastic can be trimmed off with a small sharp scissors.

# Pattern Design

Bear in mind that your grid charted pattern has the rectangles colored in vertical patterns. Each rectangle equals one bead. Your beads will actually lay on a diagonal. Expect some shifting and variation of your charted pattern.

The beauty of beading on counted canvas is that any grid design can be used for beading. Of course, challenge yourself to make your own patterns. You can get ideas from needlepoint, cross stitch, or machine knitting patterns.

Make photo copies of the graph paper on the next page. You can splice several together for large patterns.

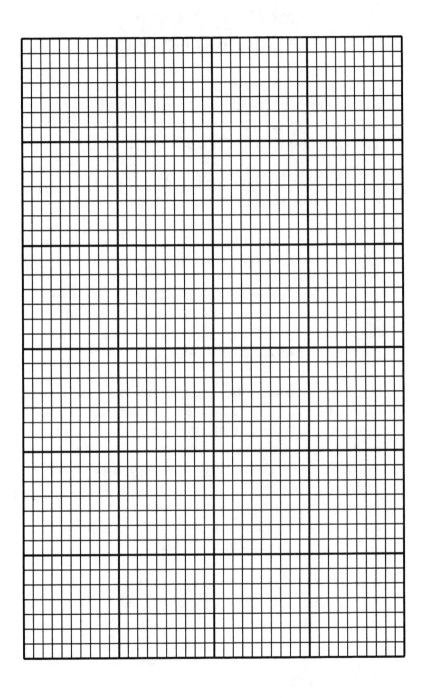

# Successful Beading
# On Counted Canvas

1. After graphing your creation, take the time to count the color and the number of beads row by row. In the margin of your graphed design, record this information as the example below. This extra effort is a real time and eye saver!
   Example:
   Row 1: 5 blue, 7 yellow, 2 blank, 4 blue
   Row 2: 2 blank, 5 blue, 9 yellow, 1 blank, 6 blue

2. Use a ruler or note card and lay the edge just under the row you are reading. You are reading line by line with a bookmark.

3. When working your patterns on counted canvas, your beads all lay in the same direction. The bead holes and beading thread run from the bottom left corner of each stitch to the top right corner of the same stitch.

4. Begin by using the following knotting technique: Using a double thread, pass the needle up to the right side of the canvas through the bottom left corner of the first stitch. Put on the first bead and pass the needle back to the wrong side through the top right hole of the stitch, leaving a 3" tail. Make a tight double knot with the tail and the working thread while keeping the bead in position. Leave the tail long, so that you may put each thread into a needle and weave it through the wrong side of this row at a later time.

5. With the needle still on the wrong side, pass it up to the right side of the canvas through the bottom left hole of the next stitch and to the right of the first stitch.

6. You now put on the next bead and pass the needle down to the wrong side as the first bead.

110

7. **Fig. 1**

Continue in this manner until you have completed this row. Then pass the needle on the wrong side to the top right corner of the first bead in row 2. The first bead in row 2 is directly above the last bead in row 1.

**Fig. 1**

8. Turn your fabric 90 degrees so that you can once again work left bottom to right top and left to right across row 2. If you have recorded a color key for the pattern, all even numbered rows will be read backwards.

9. When ending a thread, knot off by passing the needle and thread under the last stitch on the wrong side of the fabric. *Pass the needle under the thread again, put the needle through the thread loop you have created and pull tightly. Repeat from the * to form a double knot which is tight and close to the fabric, leaving a 3" tail. Then thread each tail on a needle, one tail at a time. Pass each tail *between* the threads on the wrong side of a completed row and the fabric. Cut off any excess tail.

**Challenges For Counted Canvas:**

1. For practice, try the charted patterns on the page 113.

2. Use clear beads and one strand of colored embroidery floss as thread. The color of the floss will become the color of the bead.     (cont'd)

**Challenges (cont'd):**

3. Make a pattern where you put on three beads at a time and cover two diagonal squares with each stitch.

4. Change the direction of your beads in some areas of your design.

5. Combine traditional thread and needlepoint, cross stitch, or embroidery stitches with bead stitches.

6. Make a second pass after finishing your counted canvas design and add texture with stitches from Trail 7.

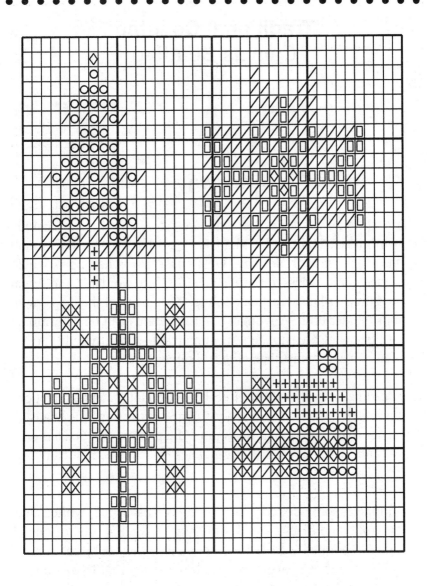

**Color Key:**

| | | | |
|---|---|---|---|
| / | Red | O | Green |
| ▯ | White | ◇ | Gold |
| X | Blue | + | Black |

● ● ● ● ● ● ● ● ● ● ● ● ● ● ● ● ● ● ● ● ● ● ● ● ● ● ●

# Traditional Counted
# Canvas Beading

# Norway

The traditional costumes from the west coast of Norway include women's beaded breast plates and beaded belts. They are only found on the west coast of Norway. West coast towns had ports which gave the people access to European beads. The woman's traditional beaded breast plate is fastened to the scoop neck of the dress, with a blouse under both. A woman's marital status can be determined by her belt and breastplate. An unmarried woman would have a beaded belt and breastplate with the same pattern.

The beading is sewn as the diagonal beaded counted canvas directions in this chapter. Each bead is sewn on one at a time and the beads all lay in the same direction. Years past, the pattern was beaded onto wool fabric without a grid for guidance, today 14 count canvas is used.

Traditionally, only six colors of beads are used: red, white, blue, green, gold, and black. The design is always composed of one or more eight pointed stars (snowflake). Numerous combinations of snowflakes sizes, repeat patterns, and colors are used. Two examples of traditional snowflake patterns are illustrated on the preceding charted pattern page.

For more information on Norwegian costumes, contact the Vesterheim Norwegian-American Museum in Decorah, Iowa. See Appendix.

# Romania

The Romanians also bead patterns on counted canvas on men's wide belts and sleeve borders and on women's vests for traditional dress and celebrations. They do not always sew all beads in the same diagonal direction. They reverse the direction of the diagonal pattern in some of the elements of their finished design. This gives more definition of the pattern and texture to their work.

Each of 20 or so Hungarian villages of the Kalotaszeg region in Transylvania, Romania favor one of three types of bead embellishment on fabric. They are: bead embroidery (beads sewn onto fabric), loom work (worked differently than we know it), and beads sewn on open weave canvas.

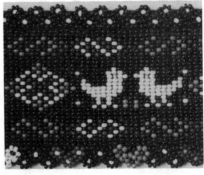

*Bead Embroidery (top left)*
*Loom Work (center right)*
*Open Weave Canvas (bottom left)*

115

**Hungarian Bojt** (tassel or pompom)
Village of Vista in northwest Romania
*Wooden form covered with yarn needle lace, bead embroidered with motifs*

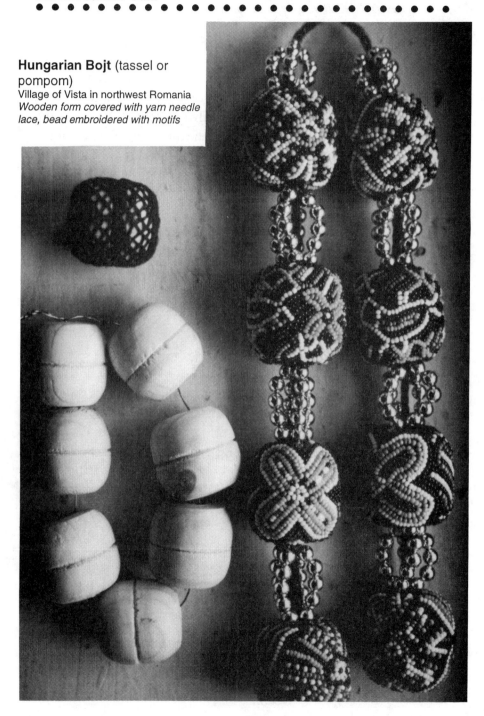

# Appendix

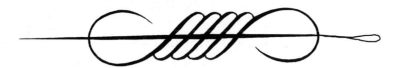

# Crazy Quilt Patchwork Techniques

## Preparing the Fabric

Pre-wash all fabric. Light weight fabrics that do not have a nap, stretch, or have a slippery surface work well. Cottons are a good choice. Velveteen and satin are useable, but are slippery. When turning under the raw edges of these fabrics, they will produce a higher elevation than the neighboring fabric. If you want a vintage Crazy Quilt look, you will be using satin and velveteen. If you use Ultra Suede or any other fabric that will not fray, you will not have to turn under edges. For fabrics with stretch, woven or knit, apply iron-on interfacing to the wrong side of the fabric before cutting the pieces.

Cut the fabric into pieces with straight edges and with variety in size, color, pattern, and shape. Your beadwork will be most dominant on solid colors of fabric.

Allow more space for the application of Crazy Beading than needed for embroidery with embroidery floss. For larger projects such as wall hangings and quilts, pieces should vary in width from 4-1/2" to

7-1/2" and be at least 18" long. For smaller projects, pieces should be no smaller than 2-1/2" on any side. Caution: Smaller pieces of fabric make it hard to do enough of a Crazy Beading stitch for it to be recognizable.

# Creating the Layout

# Basting Method

On medium or heavy weight muslin, mark the desired finished size of your Crazy Quilt piece. For any project larger than your hand, you will need to leave a muslin border wide enough to anchor to a canvas stretcher or use in a large hoop. It is much easier to Crazy Bead when the fabric is kept flat.

1. Starting at one edge of the marked muslin, pin the first fabric piece in place. This piece will have no fold under edges. The second piece will overlap one edge of the first piece. This edge should overlap approximately 1/2" and be *folded under 1/2"* or less as it is pinned into place.

2. Continue building the layout outward from the pieces that are pinned in place. Some pieces will need to be *folded under on two or more edges*. Take your time exploring and constructing your layout.

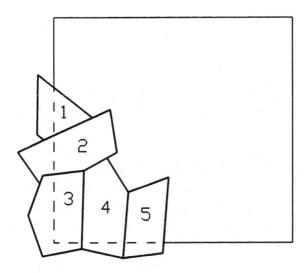

3. Neighboring pieces should contrast in color, size, pattern, and shape. On the outer edges, portions of the fabric pieces may go over the lines of the marked muslin pattern outline. Trim the excess off after you are done basting all the pieces into place.

4. After pinning all pieces to the muslin base, baste pieces into place. Baste through all three layers near the folds on all folded edges. (Muslin and folded layers) Machine or hand baste being careful that all raw edges remain folded under. Remove pins. Baste the edges to muslin on the marked pattern line. Cut off the excess fabric raw edges leaving an additional 1/4" of fabric past the marked pattern line on the muslin.

5. Attach to canvas stretcher or insert in large hoop, keeping fabric taut. Begin Crazy Beading.

● ● ● ● ● ● ● ● ● ● ● ● ● ● ● ● ● ● ● ● ● ● ● ● ● ● ●

# Fusible Webbing: No Sew Method

*Wonder-Under is a registered trademark of Freudenberg Nonwovens.*

Fusible webbing can be fused to the wrong side of any fabric that can be pressed with a hot iron. The fusible webbing will prevent cut edges from unraveling.

Wonder-Under is a double sided fusible webbing you can purchase at most fabric stores. Follow the manufacturer's directions on fusing Wonder-Under to the wrong side of your fabric *before* cutting into pieces. Continue by following the directions on Preparing the Fabric which can be found in the first paragraph of Crazy Quilt Patchwork Techniques at the beginning of the Appendix. Keep in mind, you do not have to allow for any folded edges with this technique.

Continue to follow the directions in Creating the Layout: Basting Method with these exceptions: Iron first piece in place on the muslin following the fusible webbing manufacturer's instructions. Slightly overlap the second piece. No folding under is needed. Iron this piece to the muslin and 1/2" or less over edge of the first piece as per the manufacturer's directions. Continue piece by piece until the pattern you drew on the muslin is covered. No need for pins, folding, or basting!

Attach to canvas stretcher or insert in a large hoop to keep fabric taut. Begin Crazy Beading.

# Canvas Stretcher Floor Stand

A floor stand on which a canvas stretcher can be clamped works well for any piece of fabric that is too large for a hoop. The fabric can be beaded unsecured, but you run the risk of rippling the fabric and distorting your desired project size and shape.

A pattern has been included for you or your favorite handyperson. If you know of no such person, the floor stand can be ordered with the order form at the back of this book.

I have not found a reasonably priced stand that can accommodate long pieces of fabric through any retail needlework source. The scroll holders sold in needleworking shops are expensive and will not work. Due to the texture of beadwork, you cannot roll or scroll beaded fabric.

With this floor stand, you can reach under and over from all sides. It will slide open to hold a canvas stretcher that is 23" to 48" long.

It is important to use a hard wood, preferably without knots for long life and a sturdy structure. To secure canvas stretcher frame to the floor stand, use "C" clamps or my favorite, 2" Quick Grip Clamps by American Tool. You will need four clamps to hold the canvas stretcher to the top of the stand cross bars.

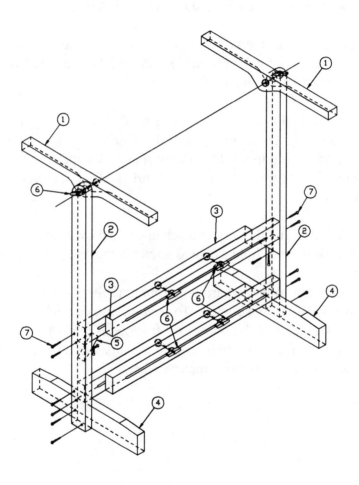

## Assembly Instructions

1. Secure Vertical Support to Floor Stand using 3/16" Phillips Screws.

2. Secure Cross Beams to Vertical Supports using 3/16" Phillips Screws.

3. Install Bracket under uppermost Cross Beam using 3/16" Phillips Screws.

4. Install Stretch Arms to Vertical Supports using ¼" hex head bolt, washers and wing-nuts.

5. Lastly install ¼" hex head bolts, washers and wing-nuts through slotted holes in Cross Beams.

| ITEM | QTY | DESCRIPTION |
|------|-----|-------------|
| 1 | 2 | Stretch Arm |
| 2 | 2 | Vertical Support |
| 3 | 4 | Cross Beam |
| 4 | 2 | Floor Stand |
| 5 | 2 | Bracket |
| 6 | 6 | Round Hd Mach Screw Slotted. 1/4"-20x2 1/2" lg. with (3) washers. |
| 7 | 16 | 3/16"∅-20x1 3/4" Lg Phillips Screw Countersunk |

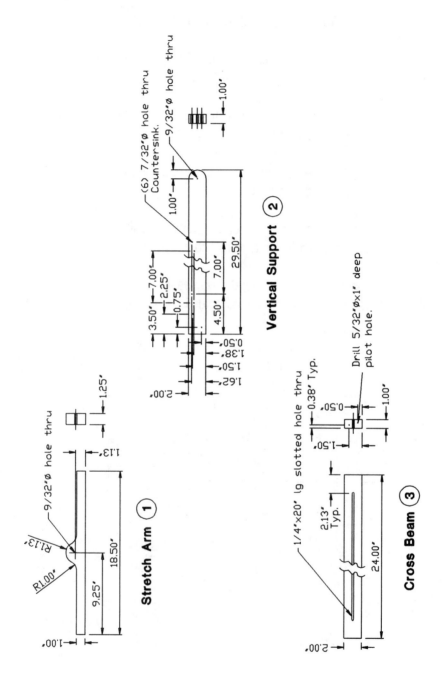

(6) 7/32"∅ hole thru
Countersink.

9/32"∅ hole thru

1.00"

1.00"

3.50"
7.00"
2.25"
0.75"

29.50"

7.00"

4.50"

2.00"
1.62"
1.50"
1.38"
0.50"

**Vertical Support** ②

9/32"∅ hole thru

1.25"

R1.13"

R1.00"

1.13"

18.50"

9.25"

1.00"

**Stretch Arm** ①

1/4"×20" lg slotted hole thru

0.38" Typ.

Drill 5/32"∅×1" deep
pilot hole.

0.50"

1.00"

1.50"

2.13"
Typ.

24.00"

2.00"

**Cross Beam** ③

124

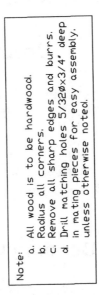

Note:
a. All wood is to be hardwood.
b. Radius all corners.
c. Remove all sharp edges and burrs.
d. Drill matching holes 5/32∅×3/4" deep in mating pieces for easy assembly, unless otherwise noted.

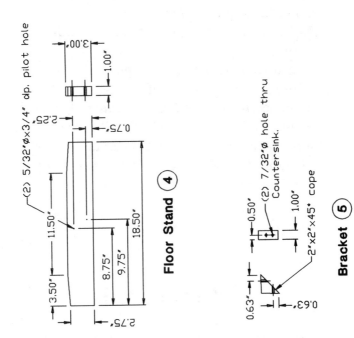

**Floor Stand ④**

**Bracket ⑤**

●●●●●●●●●●●●●●●●●●●●●●●●●●●●●●

# Suggested Reading/Bibliography

## Creativity

Bayles, David and Orland, Ted, *Art and Fear,* Kapra, 1994.

Burns, MD, David, *Feeling Good: The New Mood Therapy,* Penguin, 1980.

Cameron, Julia, *The Artist's Way: A Spiritual Path to Higher Creativity,* Tarcher/Putnam, 1992.

Edwards, Betty, *Drawing On The Right Side of The Brain*, Putnam, 1989.

## Beading On Fabric

Blakelock, Virginia, *Those Bad Bad Beads,* Self Published, 1990 (Available from Universal Synergetics).

Campbell-Harding, Valerie and Watts, Pamela, *Bead Embroidery,* Lacis, 1993.

Edwards, Joan, *Bead Embroidery*, Taplinger, 1967.

Ettinger, Roseann, *Handbags,* Shiffer, 1991.

Goodhue, Horace, *Indian Beadweaving Patterns,* Bead-Craft, 1989.

Moss, Kathlyn and Shere, Alice, *The New Beadwork,* Abrams, 1992.

Scott, Joyce, *Fearless Beadwork,* Visual Studies Workshop, 1994.

Spears, Therese, *Beaded Clothing Techniques,* Promenade, 1984.

Woodsmall, Annabel Whitney, *Contemporary Appliquéd Beadwork,* HTH, 1979.

## Needlework

Cartwright-Jones, Catherine, *Tap-Dancing Lizards,* Interweave, 1992. (Machine knitting patterns)

● ● ● ● ● ● ● ● ● ● ● ● ● ● ● ● ● ● ● ● ● ● ● ● ●

Dettore, Arlene and Maxwell, Beverly, *Victorian Patchwork and Quilting,* Meredith Press, 1995.

Montano, Judith, *The Crazy Quilt Handbook,* C & T, 1986.

Montano, Judith, *Elegant Stitches,* C & T, 1995.

Wood, Dorothy, *50 Victorian Needlecraft Designs,* Anness, 1995.

# Magazines

Available at bookstores:
*Bead and Button*
*Intuition*
*Lapidary Journal*
*New Age Journal*
*Ornament*
*Quilter's Newsletter Magazine*
*Threads*

# Cyber Bead Sites

(Bead Societies, bead shops, beadwork, idea exchanges)
http://www.thebeadsite.com
http://www.mcs.net/~simone
http://www.aa.net/~beadart/
http://www.beadwrangler.com
http:/www.nfobase.com    (The Bead Bugle)
News Groups: alt.beadworld, rec.crafts.beads,
rec.crafts.textiles.sewing

● ● ● ● ● ● ● ● ● ● ● ● ● ● ● ● ● ● ● ● ● ● ● ● ● ● ● ● ●

# Supplies

## Beads

*Fire Mountain Gems*
28195 Redwood Highway Road, Cave Junction, OR 97523
(888) 347-3436

*Out On A Whim*
121 E. Cotati Avenue, Cotati, CA 94931
(800) BEAD-111

*Rings & Things*
PO Box 450, Spokane, WA 99210
(800) 366-2154

*Universal Synergetics*
16510 SW Edminston Road, Wilsonville, OR 97070
(503) 625-2323

## Silamide Thread

*Universal Synergetics* (see above)

The service and supplies from the above sources have been consistently excellent. Please also consider purchasing from your local suppliers. If you don't support them, they may not be in business when you need them. Look up "Beads" in your yellow pages phone directory.

# Ultra Suede

*Ultra Suede is a registered trademark of Springs Industries, Inc.*

*Baer Fabrics*
515 E. Market Street, Louisville, KY 40202
(800) 769-7776
100 ULS samples $9.50, refundable with order.

*Curran Square Fabrics*
6823 Redmond Drive, McLean, VA 22101
(703) 556-9292
Swatching available

*G Street Fabrics*
12240 Wilkins Avenue, Rockville, MD 20852
(800) 333-9191
100 ULS swatches $10, refundable with order.

# PVC Plastic Sheets

Sold as *Sheet Plastic for Quilters* in quilt shops.
Made by: Inglis Products
Box 400, Chelsea, MI 48118

# Canvas Stretcher

Art supply stores

# Selected Glossary

**Baste** Long hand or machine sewn stitches. Basting stitches are usually temporary and removed when the project is completed.

**Bugle bead** A tubular glass bead. It can vary in length from 1/8" to 2".

**Edging** A series of beaded strands in a row which are joined by additional beads at or near the end of the strands. The edging stitches are anchored by their base to the fabric. Traditionally sewn on the hem or through a fold on the edge of the fabric.

**Fringe** A series of beaded strands that hang from the fabric independently or semi-independently from each other.

**Quilt** Traditionally consisting of three layers sewn together: top fabric, batting, and back fabric.

**Quilting** The act of hand or machine sewing a pattern through all three quilt layers.

**Raw Edges** The cut edges of a piece of fabric.

**Right side of fabric** The side of the fabric that you will look at when the project is completed. Your beadwork will be on this side.

**Seed bead** Small glass beads which are roundish in shape. Sized according to number. The higher the number, the smaller the bead. The degree sign is placed in front of the number or after the number to indicate the bead size.

**Stop bead** The bead that stops your bead formation from falling off of the thread or fabric.

**Tension** How tight thread or fabric is pulled or stretched.

**Wrong side of fabric** The side of the fabric you will not see when your project is completed. The knots and most of your thread stitches will be on this side.

● ● ● ● ● ● ● ● ● ● ● ● ● ● ● ● ● ● ● ● ● ● ● ● ● ● ● ● ● ●

# Acknowledgements

I sincerely thank all these fine people for their contributions to this work:

My thirteen fearless "Test Beaders" who provided me with written and beaded evaluations of the first draft: Karen Salsbury, Cindy Reiland, Candice Christensen, Cheryl Erickson, Alois Powers, Beatrice Pieper, Pam Videen, Barbara Bach, Theresa Leahy, Angela Heyer, Paula Heitzman, Jo Wood, and Sue Swanson.

Karen Salsbury my editing coach and ever encouraging cheerleader.

Karen Fitzgerald for her skillful graphics and illustrations. Chapter heading illustrations were produced with modified clip art from Corel Print House.

Diane Swanson for her patience and adept skill in the stylizing and final editing. This book was formatted in PageMaker 5.0.

Photo Credits:
Robin Atkins: Pages 36, 103, 115, 116
Candice Christensen: Front Cover
Nancy Eha: Back Cover, Pages 15, 76, 81, 94, 101, 112
Kelly Johnson: Pages 3, 60
Kae Krueger: Pages 4, 51, 63, 100, 106
Deborah Sproule: Page 104
Bonnie Voelker: Page 97
Jo Wood: Page 16

# Ideas and Inspirations

# Order Form

**At Last** — a versatile needlework floor stand that meets your needlework and comfort needs. Now you can have a sturdy, hardwood stand that accommodates your work up to 48" wide, unlimited length — with no interference to stitches or embellishments. And with adjustable tilt, you can sit and work comfortably.

**Easy to assemble kit.**

Mail check or
money order to:

**NeedleWerks**
10845 Thrush Street N.W.
Coon Rapids, MN 55433

Name _____

Address _____

City _____ State _____ ZIP_____

Quantity _____ @$119.95 each = $ _____

Shipping and handling @ $9.95 each = $ _____

Quantity _____ @ $7.80 tax for MN residents $ _____

Total $ _____

Allow 3 to 6 weeks for delivery.

# Order Form
## Off The Beadin' Path and Beadaholic T-Shirts

**Certified Beadaholic T-Shirts**
American Made Heavy Weight 100% Cotton Short Sleeve T-Shirts
Natural cotton color with full chest five color print of your favorite beads!
**Available in adult sizes: L, XL, XXL, XXXL**

| <u>Size</u> | <u>Chest Measurement of Shirt</u> | <u>Send Check or Money Order To:</u> |
|------|------|------|
| Large | 44 inches | Creative Visions Press |
| X Large | 48 inches | 3898 Dellview Avenue |
| 2X Large | 52 inches | St. Paul, MN 55112 |
| 3X Large | 56 inches | |

_____ **Off The Beadin' Path @ $19.95/copy = $** _____

_____ Large T-Shirts _____X Large T-Shirts @ $18.00 = $ _____

_____2X Large T-Shirts _____3X Large T-Shirts @ $21.00 = $ _____

Shipping: $3.00 1st item = $ _____

Each Additional: $2.00 = $ _____

Sales Tax: MN residents add $1.29/book = $ _____

Total $ _____

___ I would like the book(s) signed for:

_____

_____

IF WE HAVE A QUESTION ABOUT
YOUR ORDER, AT WHAT NUMBER
CAN WE REACH YOU?

( ) _____

Ship to:

_____

_____

_____

# Order Form
## <u>Off The Beadin' Path</u> and Beadaholic T-Shirts

### Certified Beadaholic T-Shirts
**American Made Heavy Weight 100% Cotton Short Sleeve T-Shirts**
**Natural cotton color with full chest five color print of your favorite beads!**
**Available in adult sizes: L, XL, XXL, XXXL**

| <u>Size</u> | <u>Chest Measurement of Shirt</u> | <u>Send Check or Money Order To:</u> |
|---|---|---|
| Large | 44 inches | Creative Visions Press |
| X Large | 48 inches | 3898 Dellview Avenue |
| 2X Large | 52 inches | St. Paul, MN 55112 |
| 3X Large | 56 inches | |

_____ **<u>Off The Beadin' Path</u>** @ **$19.95/copy** = $ _____

_____ Large T-Shirts _____ X Large T-Shirts @ $18.00 = $ _____

_____ 2X Large T-Shirts _____ 3X Large T-Shirts @ $21.00 = $ _____

Shipping: $3.00 1st item = $ _____

Each Additional: $2.00 = $ _____

Sales Tax: MN residents add $1.29/book = $ _____

Total $ _____

___ I would like the book(s) signed for:

_____

_____

IF WE HAVE A QUESTION ABOUT
YOUR ORDER, AT WHAT NUMBER
CAN WE REACH YOU?

(    ) _____

Ship to:

_____

_____

_____

_____